Cram101 Textbook Outlines to accompany:

Essentials of International Relations

Mingst, 2nd Edition

An Academic Internet Publishers (AIPI) publication (c) 2007.

You have a discounted membership at www.Cram101.com with this book.

Get all of the practice tests for the chapters of this textbook, and access in-depth reference material for writing essays and papers. Here is an example from a Cram101 Biology text:

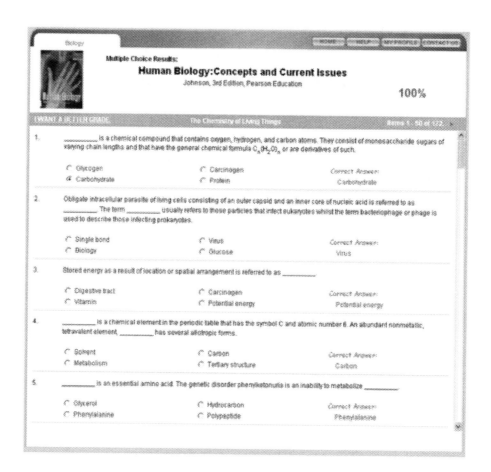

When you need problem solving help with math, stats, and other disciplines, www.Cram101.com will walk through the formulas and solutions step by step.

With Cram101.com online, you also have access to extensive reference material.

You will nail those essays and papers. Here is an example from a Cram101 Biology text:

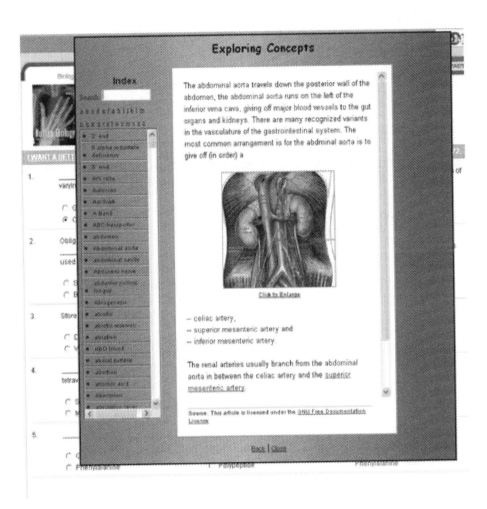

Learning System

Cram101 Textbook Outlines is a learning system. The notes in this book are the highlights of your textbook, you will never have to highlight a book again.

How to use this book. Take this book to class, it is your notebook for the lecture. The notes and highlights on the left hand side of the pages follow the outline and order of the textbook. All you have to do is follow along while your intructor presents the lecture. Circle the items emphasized in class and add other important information on the right side. With Cram101 Textbook Outlines you'll spend less time writing and more time listening. Learning becomes more efficient.

Cram101.com Online

Increase your studying efficiency by using Cram101.com's practice tests and online reference material. It is the perfect complement to Cram101 Textbook Outlines. Use self-teaching matching tests or simulate in-class testing with comprehensive multiple choice tests, or simply use Cram's true and false tests for quick review. Cram101.com even allows you to enter your in-class notes for an integrated studying format combining the textbook notes with your class notes.

Visit **www.Cram101.com**, click Sign Up at the top of the screen, and enter **DK73DW1926** in the promo code box on the registration screen. Access to www.Cram101.com is normally $9.95, but because you have purchased this book, your access fee is only $4.95. Sign up and stop highlighting textbooks forever.

Essentials of International Relations
Mingst, 2nd

CONTENTS

International relations	International relations a branch of political science, is the study of foreign relations and global issues among states within the international system, including the roles of states, inter-governmental organizations, non-governmental organizations, and multinational corporations. It is both an academic and public policy field, and can be either positive or normative as it both seeks to analyze as well as formulate the foreign policy of particular states.
Behavioralism	Behavioralism is an approach in political science which seeks to provide an objective, quantified approach to explaining and predicting political behavior. It is associated with the rise of the behavioral sciences, modeled after the natural sciences.
Corporation	A corporation is an artificial legal entity which, while made up of a number of natural persons or other legal entities, has a separate legal identity from them. As a legal entity the corporation receives legal rights and duties
Multinational corporation	A multinational corporation is a corporation or enterprise that manages production establishments or delivers services in at least two countries. Very large multinationals have budgets that exceed those of many countries. They can have a powerful influence in international relations and local economies.
Trade organization	Trade organization is generally a public relations organization founded and funded by corporations that operate in a specific industry. Its purpose is generally to promote the industry through PR activities such as advertizing, education, political donations, lobbying and publishing.
World Trade Organization	World Trade Organization is an international organization designed to supervise and liberalize international trade. The WTO came into being on January 1, 1995, and is the successor to the General Agreement on Tariffs and Trade, which was created in 1947, and continued to operate for almost five decades as a de facto international organization.
Human nature	Human nature is the fundamental nature and substance of humans, as well as the range of human behavior that is, believed to be invariant over long periods of time and across very different cultural contexts.
Marxism	Marxism of Karl Marx and Friedrich Engels. Any political practice or theory that is based on an interpretation of the works of Marx and Engels may be termed Marxism.
Reasons of state	The reasons of state is a country's goals and ambitions whether economic, military, or cultural. The notion is an important one in international relations where pursuit of the national interest is the foundation of the realist school.
Radicalism	Radicalism is a political movement for those favouring or trying to produce thoroughgoing political reforms which can include changes to the social order to a greater or lesser extent toward the right.
Postmodernism	The term Postmodernism was coined in 1949 to describe a dissatisfaction with modern architecture, founding the postmodern architecture, and later of, relating to, or being any of several movements.
Orthodoxy	The word **orthodoxy** , from the Greek ortho and doxa, is typically used to refer to the correct worship or the correct theological and doctrinal observance of religion, as determined by some overseeing body.
Cold War	The Cold War was the period of conflict, tension and competition between the United States and the Soviet Union and their respective allies from the mid-1940s until the early 1990s.
Diplomacy	Diplomacy is the art and practice of conducting negotiations between representatives of groups or states. It usually refers to international diplomacy, the conduct of international relations through the intercession of professional diplomats with regard to issues of peace-making, trade, war, economics and culture. International treaties are usually negotiated by diplomats prior to endorsement by national politicians.
Economic Growth	Economic growth is the increase in value of the goods and services produced by an economy. It is conventionally measured as the percent rate of increase in real gross domestic product, or GDP. Growth is usually calculated in real terms, i.e. inflation-adjusted terms, in order to net out the effect of

inflation on the price of the goods and services produced.

Economism	Economism is a term used to criticize economic reductionism, that is the reduction of all social facts to economical dimensions. It is also used to criticize economics as an ideology, in which supply and demand are the only important factors in decisions, and literally outstrip or permit ignoring all other factors.
Appeasement	**Appeasement** is a policy of accepting the imposed conditions of an aggressor in lieu of armed resistance, usually at the sacrifice of principles. Since World War II, the term has gained a negative connotation in the British government, in politics and in general, of weakness, cowardice and self-deception.
Republic	A republic is a form of government maintained by a state or country whose sovereignty is based on popular consent and whose governance is based on popular representation and control. Several definitions stress the importance of the rule of law as among the requirements for a republic.
Anarchism	Anarchism is a political philosophy or group of doctrines and attitudes centered on rejection of any form of compulsory government and supporting its elimination. Thus anarchism, in its most general meaning, is the belief that all forms of rulership and thus also involuntary servitude are undesirable and should be abolished.
Cosmopolitanism	Cosmopolitanism is the idea that all of humanity belongs to a single moral community. This is contrasted with ideologies of patriotism and nationalism. Cosmopolitanism may or may not entail some sort of world government or it may simply refer to more inclusive moral, economic, and/or political relationships between nations or individuals of different nations[citation needed].
Universalism	Universalism refers to any concept or doctrine that applies to all persons and/or all things for all times and in all situations.
Natural law	Natural law is an ethical theory that posits the existence of a law whose content is set by nature and that therefore has validity everywhere. The phrase natural law is sometimes opposed to the positive law of a given political community, society, or nation-state, and can thus function as a standard by which to criticize that law.
Social contract	The term social contract describes a broad class of philosophical theories whose subject is the implied agreements by which people form nations and maintain social order.
Rule of law	The rule of law is the principle that governmental authority is legitimately exercized only in accordance with written, publicly disclosed laws adopted and enforced in accordance with established procedure.
Township	A township is a settlement which has been granted the status and powers of a unit of local government. Specific use of the term to describe political subdivisions has varied by country.
Scientific method	**Scientific method** is a body of techniques for investigating phenomena and acquiring new knowledge, as well as for correcting and integrating previous knowledge. It is based on gathering observable, empirical, measurable evidence, subject to specific principles of reasoning.
Sovereignty	Sovereignty is the exclusive right to exercise supreme political authority over a geographic region, group of people, or oneself. The source or justification of sovereignty ("by God" or "by people") must be distinguished from its exercise by branches of government. In democratic states, sovereignty is held by the people.
Treaty	A treaty is an agreement under international law entered into by actors in international law, namely states and international organizations. Under United States constitutional law, only a treaty that has achieved advice and consent of two-thirds of the Senate present is properly designated as a treaty.
National security	National security refers to the requirement to maintain the survival of the nation-state through the use of economic, military and political power and the exercise of diplomacy.

Go to **Cram101.com** for the Practice Tests for this Chapter.

Foreign policy	A country's foreign policy is a set of political goals that seeks to outline how that particular country will interact with other countries of the world and, to a lesser extent, non-state actors. They generally are designed to help protect a country's national interests, national security, ideological goals, and economic prosperity.
Political economy	Political economy was the original term for the study of production, the acts of buying and selling, and their relationships to laws, customs and government. It developed in the 18th century as the study of the economies of states.

Go to **Cram101.com** for the Practice Tests for this Chapter.

Go to **Cram101.com** for the Practice Tests for this Chapter.
And, **NEVER** highlight a book again!

International relations	International relations a branch of political science, is the study of foreign relations and global issues among states within the international system, including the roles of states, inter-governmental organizations, non-governmental organizations, and multinational corporations. It is both an academic and public policy field, and can be either positive or normative as it both seeks to analyze as well as formulate the foreign policy of particular states.
Treaty	A treaty is an agreement under international law entered into by actors in international law, namely states and international organizations. Under United States constitutional law, only a treaty that has achieved advice and consent of two-thirds of the Senate present is properly designated as a treaty.
Cold War	The Cold War was the period of conflict, tension and competition between the United States and the Soviet Union and their respective allies from the mid-1940s until the early 1990s.
Sovereignty	Sovereignty is the exclusive right to exercise supreme political authority over a geographic region, group of people, or oneself. The source or justification of sovereignty ("by God" or "by people") must be distinguished from its exercise by branches of government. In democratic states, sovereignty is held by the people.
Sphere of influence	A sphere of influence is an area or region over which an organization or state exerts some kind of indirect cultural, economic, military or political domination. Also, in some areas of habitation, shopping or retail outlets or indeed destination outlets, have a sphere of influence over towns of certain areas, for example the Central Business District.
Bureaucrat	A bureaucrat is a member of a bureaucracy, usually within an institution of the government.
Citizenship	Citizenship is membership in a political community and carries with it rights to political participation; a person having such membership is a citizen. It is largely coterminous with nationality, although it is possible to have a nationality without being a citizen ; it is also possible to have political rights without being a national of a state.
Autonomy	Autonomy means freedom from external authority. In politics, autonomy refers to self-governance.
Decentralization	Decentralization is the process of dispersing decision-making closer to the point of service or action. It occurs in a great many contexts in engineering, management science, political science, political economy, sociology and economics — each of which could be said to study mass decision-making by groups, too large to consult with each other very directly.
Feudalism	**Feudalism** refers to a general set of reciprocal legal and military obligations among the warrior nobility of Europe during the Middle Ages, revolving around the three key concepts of lords, vassals, and fiefs.
Universalism	Universalism refers to any concept or doctrine that applies to all persons and/or all things for all times and in all situations.
Diplomacy	Diplomacy is the art and practice of conducting negotiations between representatives of groups or states. It usually refers to international diplomacy, the conduct of international relations through the intercession of professional diplomats with regard to issues of peace-making, trade, war, economics and culture. International treaties are usually negotiated by diplomats prior to endorsement by national politicians.
Imperialism	Imperialism is the policy of extending a nation's authority by territorial acquisition or by the establishment of economic and political hegemony over other nations, countries, or colonies. This is realized either through direct territorial conquest or settlement, or through indirect methods of influencing or controlling the politics and/or economy.
Monarchy	A **monarchy** , from the Greek ïïíïò, "one", and áñ÷åí, "to rule', is a form of government

Go to **Cram101.com** for the Practice Tests for this Chapter.

9

that has a monarch as head of state. In most monarchies the monarch usually reigns as head of state for life; this is also true in many republics, though it is also common for the Head of State (often called the president) to be elected for a certain amount of time. There are currently 32 monarchs reigning over 46 extant sovereign monarchies in the world, the monarch of the United Kingdom being shared with 15 other independent realms. As such, this one multiple monarch reigns over vast geographic areas including the trans-continental realms of Canada and Australia. Only one, Andorra, is ruled by two co-monarchs.

Commonwealth	Commonwealth originally meant a state governed for the common good as opposed to an authoritarian state governed for the benefit of a given class of owners. Today the term is more general and means a political community.
Natural law	Natural law is an ethical theory that posits the existence of a law whose content is set by nature and that therefore has validity everywhere. The phrase natural law is sometimes opposed to the positive law of a given political community, society, or nation-state, and can thus function as a standard by which to criticize that law.
Aristocracy	The term aristocracy refers to a form of government where power is hereditary, and split between a small number of families. Aristocracy can also refer to the highest class in society even if they do not rule directly.
Democracy	Democracy is a form of government in which supreme power is vested in the people and exercised by them directly or indirectly through a system of representation usually involving periodic free elections.
Capitalism	Capitalism generally refers to an economic system in which the means of production are mostly privately owned and operated for profit, and in which distribution, production and pricing of goods and services are determined in a largely free market. It is usually considered to involve the right of individuals and groups of individuals acting as "legal persons" or corporations to trade capital goods, labor, land and money.
Social contract	The term social contract describes a broad class of philosophical theories whose subject is the implied agreements by which people form nations and maintain social order.
Divine right	The Divine Right of Kings is a European political and religious doctrine of political absolutism. Such doctrines are largely, though not exclusively, associated with the medieval and ancien régime eras. It states that a monarch owes his rule to the will of God, and not necessarily to the will of his subjects, the aristocracy or any other competing authority, implying that any attempt to depose him or to restrict his powers runs contrary to the will of God.
Natural rights	Natural rights are universal rights that are seen as inherent in the nature of people and not contingent on human actions or beliefs. One theory of natural rights was developed from the theory of natural law during the Enlightenment in opposition to the divine right of kings, and provided a moral justification for liberalism.
Legitimacy	Legitimacy in political science, is the popular acceptance of a governing regime or law as an authority. Where as authority refers to a specific position in an established government, the term legitimacy is used when describing a system of government itself —where "government may be generalized to mean the wider "sphere of influence."
Consent of the governed	" Consent of the governed " is a political theory stating that a government's legitimacy and moral right to use state power is, or ought to be, derived from the people or society over which that power is exercized. This theory of "consent" is historically contrasted to the divine right of kings and has often been invoked against the legitimacy of colonialism.
Nationalism	Nationalism, in its broadest sense, is a devotion to one's own nation and its interests over those of all other nations. The term can also refer to a doctrine or political movement

Go to **Cram101.com** for the Practice Tests for this Chapter.

	that holds that a nation—usually defined in terms of ethnicity or culture—has the right to constitute an independent or autonomous political community based on a shared history and common destiny.
Republic	A republic is a form of government maintained by a state or country whose sovereignty is based on popular consent and whose governance is based on popular representation and control. Several definitions stress the importance of the rule of law as among the requirements for a republic.
Annexation	Annexation is the legal incorporation of some territory into another geo-political entity. Usually, it is implied that the territory and population being annexed is the smaller, more peripheral or weaker of the two merging entities. It can also imply a certain measure of coercion, expansionism or unilateralism on the part of the stronger of the merging entities. Because of this, more positive words like political union or reunification are sometimes preferred.
Industrializ-tion	Industrialisation (also spelt **Industrialization**) or an Industrial Revolution is a process of social and economic change whereby a human society is transformed from a pre-industrial to an industrial state.
Industrial Revolution	The **Industrial Revolution** was a major shift of technological, socioeconomic, and cultural conditions in the mid 18th century and early 19th century. It began in Britain and spread throughout the world.
Balance of power	Balance of power refers to the division, distribution, or separation of powers within a national political system.
Foreign policy	A country's foreign policy is a set of political goals that seeks to outline how that particular country will interact with other countries of the world and, to a lesser extent, non-state actors. They generally are designed to help protect a country's national interests, national security, ideological goals, and economic prosperity.
Chancellor	Chancellor an official title used by most of the peoples whose civilization has arisen directly or indirectly out of the Roman Empire. At different times and in different countries it has stood for various duties and has been borne by officers of various degrees of dignity. Various governments have a chancellor who serves as some form of junior or senior minister.
Diplomatic recognition	Diplomatic recognition is a political act by which one state acknowledges an act or status of another state or government, thereby according it legitimacy and expressing its intent to bring into force the domestic and international legal consequences of recognition.
Conservativism	Conservativism is a relativistic term used to describe political philosophies that favor traditional values, where "tradition" refers to religious, cultural, or nationally defined beliefs and customs.
Ideology	An ideology is an organized collection of ideas. The word ideology was coined by Count Antoine Destutt de Tracy in the late 18th century to define a "science of ideas." An ideology can be thought of as a comprehensive vision, as a way of looking at things, as in common sense and several philosophical tendencies, or a set of ideas proposed by the dominant class of a society to all members of this society.
Utopia	**Utopia** is an imaginary island, depicted by Sir Thomas More as a perfect social, legal, and political system. It may be used pejoratively, to refer to a society that is unrealistic and impossible to realize. It has also been used to describe actual communities founded in attempts to create an ideal society.
Fascism	Fascism is an authoritarian political ideology (generally tied to a mass movement) that considers individual and other societal interests inferior to the needs of the state, and seeks to forge a type of national unity, usually based on ethnic, religious, cultural, or

Go to **Cram101.com** for the Practice Tests for this Chapter.

racial attributes.

Redistricting	Redistricting is the changing of political borders. Often this means changing electoral district and constituency boundaries, usually in response to periodic census results. This takes place by law or constitution at least every decade in most representative democracy systems using first-past-the-post or similar electoral systems to prevent geographic malapportionment.
Prime minister	A prime minister is the most senior minister of a cabinet in the executive branch of government in a parliamentary system.
United Nations	The United Nations is an international organization whose stated aims are to facilitate co-operation in international law, international security, economic development, social progress and human rights issues.
Superpower	A superpower is a state with a leading position in the international system and the ability to influence events and project power on a worldwide scale; it is considered a higher level of power than a great power.
Containment	Containment refers to the foreign policy strategy of the United States in the early years of the Cold War in which it was to stop what it called the domino effect of nations moving politically towards Soviet Union-based communism, rather than European-American-based capitalism.
Doctrine	Doctrine is a body of axioms fundamental to the exercise of a nation's foreign policy. Hence, doctrine, in this sense, has come to suggest a broad consistency that holds true across a spectrum of acts and actions.
Truman Doctrine	The Truman Doctrine was a proclamation by president Harry S. Truman on March 12, 1947. It stated that the U.S. would support Greece and Turkey with economic and military aid to prevent their falling into the Soviet sphere. The Doctrine shifted American foreign policy as regards the Soviet Union from Détente to, as George F. Kennan phrased it, a policy of containment of Soviet expansion. Historians often use it to mark the starting date of the Cold War.
Free trade	Free trade is a market model in which trade in goods and services between or within countries flows unhindered by government-imposed restrictions. Restrictions to trade include taxes and other legislation, such as tariff and non-tariff trade barriers.
Marxism	Marxism of Karl Marx and Friedrich Engels. Any political practice or theory that is based on an interpretation of the works of Marx and Engels may be termed Marxism.
Proletariat	The **proletariat** is a term used to identify a lower social class; a member of such a class is proletarian. Originally it was identified as those people who had no wealth other than their sons; the term was initially used in a derogatory sense, until Karl Marx used it as a sociological term to refer to the working class.
Socialism	Socialism refers to a broad array of doctrines or political movements that envisage a socio-economic system in which property and the distribution of wealth are subject to control by the community.
Marshall Plan	The Marshall Plan was the primary plan of the United States for rebuilding and creating a stronger foundation for the allied countries of Europe, and repelling communism after World War II.
Communism	Communism is an ideology that seeks to establish a classless, stateless social organization based on common ownership of the means of production. It can be considered a branch of the broader socialist movement. Communism as a political goal is generally a conjectured form of future social organization, although Marxists have described early forms of human social

Go to **Cram101.com** for the Practice Tests for this Chapter.

organization as 'primitive communism'.

Globalization	Globalization is an umbrella term and is perhaps best understood as a unitary process inclusive of many sub-processes (such as enhanced economic interdependence, increased cultural influence, rapid advances of information technology, and novel governance and geopolitical challenges) that are increasingly binding people and the biosphere more tightly into one global system.
Communist Party	In modern usage, the term communist party is generally used to identify any political party which has adopted communist ideology. However, the Leninist concept of a communist party includes not only ideological orientation, but also a wide set of organizational policies.
Economism	Economism is a term used to criticize economic reductionism, that is the reduction of all social facts to economical dimensions. It is also used to criticize economics as an ideology, in which supply and demand are the only important factors in decisions, and literally outstrip or permit ignoring all other factors.
New International Economic Order	The New International Economic Order (NIEO) was a set of proposals put forward during the 1970s by developing countries through the United Nations Conference on Trade and Development to promote their interests by improving their terms of trade, increasing development assistance, developed-country tariff reductions, and other means.
Reasons of state	The reasons of state is a country's goals and ambitions whether economic, military, or cultural. The notion is an important one in international relations where pursuit of the national interest is the foundation of the realist school.
Cuban Missile Crisis	The Cuban Missile Crisis was a confrontation during the Cold War between the Government of the United States, the Government of the Soviet Union, and the Government of Cuba. This crisis is generally regarded as the moment when the Cold War came closest to escalating into a nuclear war.
Deterrence	Deterrence theory is a military strategy developed after and used throughout the Cold War and current times. It is especially relevant with regard to the use of nuclear weapons, and figures prominently on current United States foreign policy regarding the development of nuclear technology in North Korea and Iran.
North Atlantic Treaty Organization	The North Atlantic Treaty Organization is a military alliance, the strongest in the world, established by the signing of the North Atlantic Treaty on April 4, 1949. With headquarters in Brussels, Belgium, the organisation established a system of collective defense whereby its member states agree to mutual defense in response to an attack by any external party, and promote liberty around the world.
Warsaw Pact	The Warsaw Pact was an organization of Central and Eastern European communist states. It was prompted by the integration of a " re-militarized" West Germany into NATO via ratification of the Paris Peace Treaties. It lasted throughout the Cold War.
Bay of pigs	The **Bay of Pigs** is an inlet on the south coast of Cuba. It is located in the province of Matanzas and is west of the city of Cienfuegos. It is where the united states planned an unsuccessful invasion by armed Cuban exiles in an attempt to overthrow the government of Fidel Castro.
Bay of Pigs invasion	The 1961 Bay of Pigs Invasion was an unsuccessful United States-planned and funded attempted invasion by armed Cuban exiles in southwest Cuba. An attempt to overthrow the government of Fidel Castro, this action accelerated a rapid deterioration in Cuban-American relations, which was further worsened by the Cuban Missile Crisis the following year.
Detente	Detente is a French term, meaning a relaxing or easing; the term has been used in international politics since the early 1970s. Generally, it may be applied to any international situation where previously hostile nations not involved in an open war "warm

up" to each other and threats de-escalate.

Reagan Doctrine	The Reagan Doctrine was an important strategy orchestrated and implemented by the United States to oppose the global influence of the Soviet Union during the final years of the Cold
Central Intelligence Agency	The Central Intelligence Agency is an intelligence agency of the United States government. Its primary function is obtaining and analyzing information about foreign governments, corporations, and persons, and reporting such information to the branches of the government.
Regime	A regime is the set of rules, both formal and informal that regulate the operation of government and its interactions with the economy and society.
Intercontinental ballistic missile	Intercontinental ballistic missile is a long-range ballistic missile typically designed for nuclear weapons delivery, that is, delivering one or more nuclear warheads.
Ballistic missile	A ballistic missile is a missile that follows a sub-orbital, ballistic flightpath with the objective of delivering a warhead to a predetermined target. The missile is only guided during the powered phase of flight and its course is governed by the laws of orbital mechanics and ballistics.
Currency	A currency is a unit of exchange, facilitating the transfer of goods and services. It is a form of money, where money is an efficient medium of exchange, and it is also considered by several people as a store of value, created through a claim to its central bank assets.
Economic Growth	Economic growth is the increase in value of the goods and services produced by an economy. It is conventionally measured as the percent rate of increase in real gross domestic product, or GDP. Growth is usually calculated in real terms, i.e. inflation-adjusted terms, in order to net out the effect of inflation on the price of the goods and services produced.
Glasnost	**Glasnost** is a Russian word for "transparency" or "openness." Mikhail Gorbachev used the term to describe a program of reform introduced to the Soviet Union in 1985 whose goals included combating corruption and the abuse of privilege by the political classes.
Perestroika	**Perestroika** , is the Russian term for the economic reforms introduced in June 1985 by the Soviet leader Mikhail Gorbachev. Its literal meaning is "restructuring", referring to the restructuring of the Soviet economy.
Command economy	Command economy is an economic system in which the state or government controls the factors of production and makes all decisions about their use and about the distribution of income.
Economic sanction	A economic sanction is a economic penalty applied by one country on another for a variety of reasons. They include, but are not limited to, tariffs, trade barriers, import duties, and import or export quotas.
Humanitarianism	Humanitarianism is an informal ideology of practice, whereby people practice humane treatment and provide assistance to others.
Coalition	A coalition is an alliance among entities, during which they cooperate in joint action, each in their own self-interest. This alliance may be temporary or a matter of convenience. A coalition government, in a parliamentary system, is a government composed of a coalition of parties.
Hegemony	Hegemony is the dominance of one group over other groups, with or without the threat of force, to the extent that, for instance, the dominant party can dictate the terms of trade to its advantage; more broadly, cultural perspectives become skewed to favor the dominant group. The cultural control that hegemony asserts affects commonplace patterns of thought: hegemony controls the way new ideas are rejected or become naturalized in a process that subtly alters notions of common sense in a given society.

International relations	International relations a branch of political science, is the study of foreign relations and global issues among states within the international system, including the roles of states, inter-governmental organizations, non-governmental organizations, and multinational corporations. It is both an academic and public policy field, and can be either positive or normative as it both seeks to analyze as well as formulate the foreign policy of particular states.
Radicalism	Radicalism is a political movement for those favouring or trying to produce thoroughgoing political reforms which can include changes to the social order to a greater or lesser extent toward the right.
Annexation	Annexation is the legal incorporation of some territory into another geo-political entity. Usually, it is implied that the territory and population being annexed is the smaller, more peripheral or weaker of the two merging entities. It can also imply a certain measure of coercion, expansionism or unilateralism on the part of the stronger of the merging entities. Because of this, more positive words like political union or reunification are sometimes preferred.
Coalition	A coalition is an alliance among entities, during which they cooperate in joint action, each in their own self-interest. This alliance may be temporary or a matter of convenience. A coalition government, in a parliamentary system, is a government composed of a coalition of parties.
Prime minister	A prime minister is the most senior minister of a cabinet in the executive branch of government in a parliamentary system.
Authoritarianism	Authoritarianism describes a form of social control characterized by strict obedience to the authority of a state or organization, often maintaining and enforcing control through the use of oppressive measures.
Marxism	Marxism of Karl Marx and Friedrich Engels. Any political practice or theory that is based on an interpretation of the works of Marx and Engels may be termed Marxism.
Democracy	Democracy is a form of government in which supreme power is vested in the people and exercised by them directly or indirectly through a system of representation usually involving periodic free elections.
Interest group	An interest group is a group, however loosely or tightly organized, doing advocacy: those determined to encourage or prevent changes in public policy without trying to be elected.
Reasons of state	The reasons of state is a country's goals and ambitions whether economic, military, or cultural. The notion is an important one in international relations where pursuit of the national interest is the foundation of the realist school.
Human nature	Human nature is the fundamental nature and substance of humans, as well as the range of human behavior that is, believed to be invariant over long periods of time and across very different cultural contexts.
Collective action	Collective action is the pursuit of a goal or set of goals by more than one person. It is a term which has formulations and theories in many areas of the social sciences.
Idealism	As an epistemological position, **Idealism** asserts that everything we experience is of a mental nature, or that we can only have direct, immediate knowledge of the contents of our mind, and can never directly know or experience an external object itself.
Civil society	Civil society is composed of the totality of voluntary civic and social organizations and institutions that form the basis of a functioning society as opposed to the force-backed structures of a state (regardless of that state's political system) and commercial institutions.

Go to **Cram101.com** for the Practice Tests for this Chapter.

Anarchism	Anarchism is a political philosophy or group of doctrines and attitudes centered on rejection of any form of compulsory government and supporting its elimination. Thus anarchism, in its most general meaning, is the belief that all forms of rulership and thus also involuntary servitude are undesirable and should be abolished.
Aristocracy	The term aristocracy refers to a form of government where power is hereditary, and split between a small number of families. Aristocracy can also refer to the highest class in society even if they do not rule directly.
Free trade	Free trade is a market model in which trade in goods and services between or within countries flows unhindered by government-imposed restrictions. Restrictions to trade include taxes and other legislation, such as tariff and non-tariff trade barriers.
Autonomy	Autonomy means freedom from external authority. In politics, autonomy refers to self-governance.
Collective security	Collective Security is a system aspiring to the maintenance of peace, in which participants agree that any "breach of the peace is to be declared to be of concern to all the participating states," 1 and will result in a collective response. This began in 1918 after the international balance of power was perceived by many nations to be no longer working correctly.
Arbitration	Arbitration is a legal technique for the resolution of disputes outside the courts, wherein the parties to a dispute refer it to one or more persons (the "arbitrators" or "arbitral tribunal"), by whose decision they agree to be bound. In the United States and other countries, the term is sometimes used in the context of describing alternative dispute resolution, a category that more commonly refers to mediation (a form of settlement negotiation facilitated by a neutral third party).
Disarmament	**Disarmament** means the act of reducing or depriving arms i.e. weaponry. Disarmament can be contrasted with "arms control," which essentially refers to the act of "controlling arms," rather than eliminating them.
Reciprocity	In international relations and treaties, the principle of reciprocity states that favours, benefits, or penalties that are granted by one state to the citizens or legal entities of another, should be returned in kind.
Human rights	Human rights refers to universal rights of people regardless of jurisdiction or other factors, such as ethnicity, age, nationality, sexual orientation or religion.
Cold War	The Cold War was the period of conflict, tension and competition between the United States and the Soviet Union and their respective allies from the mid-1940s until the early 1990s.
Interdependence	Interdependence is a dynamic of being mutually responsible to and sharing a common set of principles with others. This concept differs distinctly from "dependence" in that an interdependent relationship implies that all participants are emotionally, economically, and/or morally "independent." Some people advocate freedom or independence as a sort of ultimate good; others do the same with devotion to one's family, community, or society. Interdependence recognizes the truth in each position and weaves them together.
Liberal democracy	Liberal democracy is a form of government. It is a representative democracy in which the ability of the elected representatives to exercise decision-making power is subject to the rule of law, and usually moderated by a constitution that emphasizes the protection of the rights and freedoms of individuals, and which places constraints on the leaders and on the extent to which the will of the majority can be exercized against the rights of minorities.
Hierarchy	Hierarchy is a system of ranking and organizing things or people, where each element of the system is subordinate to a single other element.

Balance of power	Balance of power refers to the division, distribution, or separation of powers within a national political system.
Deterrence	Deterrence theory is a military strategy developed after and used throughout the Cold War and current times. It is especially relevant with regard to the use of nuclear weapons, and figures prominently on current United States foreign policy regarding the development of nuclear technology in North Korea and Iran.
Unitary State	A Unitary State is a state or country that is governed constitutionally as one single unit, with one constitutionally created legislature. The political power of government in such states may well be transferred to lower levels, to regionally or locally elected assemblies, governors and mayors, but the central government retains the principal right to recall such delegated power.
Foreign policy	A country's foreign policy is a set of political goals that seeks to outline how that particular country will interact with other countries of the world and, to a lesser extent, non-state actors. They generally are designed to help protect a country's national interests, national security, ideological goals, and economic prosperity.
Containment	Containment refers to the foreign policy strategy of the United States in the early years of the Cold War in which it was to stop what it called the domino effect of nations moving politically towards Soviet Union-based communism, rather than European-American-based capitalism.
Sphere of influence	A sphere of influence is an area or region over which an organization or state exerts some kind of indirect cultural, economic, military or political domination. Also, in some areas of habitation, shopping or retail outlets or indeed destination outlets, have a sphere of influence over towns of certain areas, for example the Central Business District.
Feudalism	**Feudalism** refers to a general set of reciprocal legal and military obligations among the warrior nobility of Europe during the Middle Ages, revolving around the three key concepts of lords, vassals, and fiefs.
Capitalism	Capitalism generally refers to an economic system in which the means of production are mostly privately owned and operated for profit, and in which distribution, production and pricing of goods and services are determined in a largely free market. It is usually considered to involve the right of individuals and groups of individuals acting as "legal persons" or corporations to trade capital goods, labor, land and money.
Proletariat	The **proletariat** is a term used to identify a lower social class; a member of such a class is proletarian. Originally it was identified as those people who had no wealth other than their sons; the term was initially used in a derogatory sense, until Karl Marx used it as a sociological term to refer to the working class.
Imperialism	Imperialism is the policy of extending a nation's authority by territorial acquisition or by the establishment of economic and political hegemony over other nations, countries, or colonies. This is realized either through direct territorial conquest or settlement, or through indirect methods of influencing or controlling the politics and/or economy.
Developed countries	The term developed countries is used to categorize countries with developed economies in which the tertiary and quaternary sectors of industry dominate. This level of economic development usually translates into a high income per capita and a high Human Development Index. Countries with high gross domestic product per capita often fit the above description of a developed economy.
Diplomacy	Diplomacy is the art and practice of conducting negotiations between representatives of groups or states. It usually refers to international diplomacy, the conduct of international relations through the intercession of professional diplomats with regard to issues of peace-

Go to **Cram101.com** for the Practice Tests for this Chapter.

making, trade, war, economics and culture. International treaties are usually negotiated by diplomats prior to endorsement by national politicians.

Corporation	A corporation is an artificial legal entity which, while made up of a number of natural persons or other legal entities, has a separate legal identity from them. As a legal entity the corporation receives legal rights and duties
Multinational corporation	A multinational corporation is a corporation or enterprise that manages production establishments or delivers services in at least two countries. Very large multinationals have budgets that exceed those of many countries. They can have a powerful influence in international relations and local economies.
Globalization	Globalization is an umbrella term and is perhaps best understood as a unitary process inclusive of many sub-processes (such as enhanced economic interdependence, increased cultural influence, rapid advances of information technology, and novel governance and geopolitical challenges) that are increasingly binding people and the biosphere more tightly into one global system.
Sovereignty	Sovereignty is the exclusive right to exercise supreme political authority over a geographic region, group of people, or oneself. The source or justification of sovereignty ("by God" or "by people") must be distinguished from its exercise by branches of government. In democratic states, sovereignty is held by the people.
Status quo	Status quo is a Latin termpresent, current, existing state of affairs. To maintain the status quo is to keep the things the way they presently are. The related phrase status quo ante, means "the state of things as it was before."
United Nations	The United Nations is an international organization whose stated aims are to facilitate co-operation in international law, international security, economic development, social progress and human rights issues.
Colonialism	Colonialism is the extension of a nation's sovereignty over territory beyond its borders by the establishment of either settler colonies or administrative dependencies in which indigenous populations are directly ruled or displaced. Colonizing nations generally dominate the resources, labor, and markets of the colonial territory, and may also impose socio-cultural, religious and linguistic structures on the conquered population (see also cultural imperialism). Though the word colonialism is often used interchangeably with imperialism, the latter is sometimes used more broadly as it covers control exercized informally (via influence) as well as formal military control or economic leverage.
Free Press	Free Press is a non-partisan, non-profit organization founded by media critic Robert McChesney to promote more democratic media policy in the United States.
Political economy	Political economy was the original term for the study of production, the acts of buying and selling, and their relationships to laws, customs and government. It developed in the 18th century as the study of the economies of states.
Mercantilism	Mercantilism is an economic theory that holds that the prosperity of a nation depends upon its supply of capital, and that the global volume of trade is "unchangeable". Economic assets, or Capital, are represented by bullion (gold, silver, and trade value) held by the state, which is best increased through a positive balance of trade with other nations (exports minus imports). Mercantilism suggests that the ruling government should advance these goals by playing a protectionist role in the economy, by encouraging exports and discouraging imports, especially through the use of tariffs. The economic policy based upon these ideas is often called the mercantile system.

Go to **Cram101.com** for the Practice Tests for this Chapter.

International relations	International relations a branch of political science, is the study of foreign relations and global issues among states within the international system, including the roles of states, inter-governmental organizations, non-governmental organizations, and multinational corporations. It is both an academic and public policy field, and can be either positive or normative as it both seeks to analyze as well as formulate the foreign policy of particular states.
United Nations	The United Nations is an international organization whose stated aims are to facilitate co-operation in international law, international security, economic development, social progress and human rights issues.
Human rights	Human rights refers to universal rights of people regardless of jurisdiction or other factors, such as ethnicity, age, nationality, sexual orientation or religion.
Corporation	A corporation is an artificial legal entity which, while made up of a number of natural persons or other legal entities, has a separate legal identity from them. As a legal entity the corporation receives legal rights and duties
Multinational corporation	A multinational corporation is a corporation or enterprise that manages production establishments or delivers services in at least two countries. Very large multinationals have budgets that exceed those of many countries. They can have a powerful influence in international relations and local economies.
Interdependence	Interdependence is a dynamic of being mutually responsible to and sharing a common set of principles with others. This concept differs distinctly from "dependence" in that an interdependent relationship implies that all participants are emotionally, economically, and/or morally "independent." Some people advocate freedom or independence as a sort of ultimate good; others do the same with devotion to one's family, community, or society. Interdependence recognizes the truth in each position and weaves them together.
Hierarchy	Hierarchy is a system of ranking and organizing things or people, where each element of the system is subordinate to a single other element.
Anarchism	Anarchism is a political philosophy or group of doctrines and attitudes centered on rejection of any form of compulsory government and supporting its elimination. Thus anarchism, in its most general meaning, is the belief that all forms of rulership and thus also involuntary servitude are undesirable and should be abolished.
National security	National security refers to the requirement to maintain the survival of the nation-state through the use of economic, military and political power and the exercise of diplomacy.
Civil society	Civil society is composed of the totality of voluntary civic and social organizations and institutions that form the basis of a functioning society as opposed to the force-backed structures of a state (regardless of that state's political system) and commercial institutions.
Autonomy	Autonomy means freedom from external authority. In politics, autonomy refers to self-governance.
Cold War	The Cold War was the period of conflict, tension and competition between the United States and the Soviet Union and their respective allies from the mid-1940s until the early 1990s.
Balance of power	Balance of power refers to the division, distribution, or separation of powers within a national political system.
North Atlantic Treaty Organization	The North Atlantic Treaty Organization is a military alliance, the strongest in the world, established by the signing of the North Atlantic Treaty on April 4, 1949. With headquarters in Brussels, Belgium, the organisation established a system of collective defense whereby its member states agree to mutual defense in response to an attack by any external party, and

	promote liberty around the world.
Treaty	A treaty is an agreement under international law entered into by actors in international law, namely states and international organizations. Under United States constitutional law, only a treaty that has achieved advice and consent of two-thirds of the Senate present is properly designated as a treaty.
Warsaw Pact	The Warsaw Pact was an organization of Central and Eastern European communist states. It was prompted by the integration of a " re-militarized" West Germany into NATO via ratification of the Paris Peace Treaties. It lasted throughout the Cold War.
Republic	A republic is a form of government maintained by a state or country whose sovereignty is based on popular consent and whose governance is based on popular representation and control. Several definitions stress the importance of the rule of law as among the requirements for a republic.
Ideology	An ideology is an organized collection of ideas. The word ideology was coined by Count Antoine Destutt de Tracy in the late 18th century to define a "science of ideas." An ideology can be thought of as a comprehensive vision, as a way of looking at things, as in common sense and several philosophical tendencies, or a set of ideas proposed by the dominant class of a society to all members of this society.
Deterrence	Deterrence theory is a military strategy developed after and used throughout the Cold War and current times. It is especially relevant with regard to the use of nuclear weapons, and figures prominently on current United States foreign policy regarding the development of nuclear technology in North Korea and Iran.
Hegemony	Hegemony is the dominance of one group over other groups, with or without the threat of force, to the extent that, for instance, the dominant party can dictate the terms of trade to its advantage; more broadly, cultural perspectives become skewed to favor the dominant group. The cultural control that hegemony asserts affects commonplace patterns of thought: hegemony controls the way new ideas are rejected or become naturalized in a process that subtly alters notions of common sense in a given society.
Political economy	Political economy was the original term for the study of production, the acts of buying and selling, and their relationships to laws, customs and government. It developed in the 18th century as the study of the economies of states.
Developed countries	The term developed countries is used to categorize countries with developed economies in which the tertiary and quaternary sectors of industry dominate. This level of economic development usually translates into a high income per capita and a high Human Development Index. Countries with high gross domestic product per capita often fit the above description of a developed economy.
Capitalism	Capitalism generally refers to an economic system in which the means of production are mostly privately owned and operated for profit, and in which distribution, production and pricing of goods and services are determined in a largely free market. It is usually considered to involve the right of individuals and groups of individuals acting as "legal persons" or corporations to trade capital goods, labor, land and money.
Economism	Economism is a term used to criticize economic reductionism, that is the reduction of all social facts to economical dimensions. It is also used to criticize economics as an ideology, in which supply and demand are the only important factors in decisions, and literally outstrip or permit ignoring all other factors.
New International Economic Order	The New International Economic Order (NIEO) was a set of proposals put forward during the 1970s by developing countries through the United Nations Conference on Trade and Development to promote their interests by improving their terms of trade, increasing development

assistance, developed-country tariff reductions, and other means.

Marxism	Marxism of Karl Marx and Friedrich Engels. Any political practice or theory that is based on an interpretation of the works of Marx and Engels may be termed Marxism.
Colonialism	Colonialism is the extension of a nation's sovereignty over territory beyond its borders by the establishment of either settler colonies or administrative dependencies in which indigenous populations are directly ruled or displaced. Colonizing nations generally dominate the resources, labor, and markets of the colonial territory, and may also impose socio-cultural, religious and linguistic structures on the conquered population (see also cultural imperialism). Though the word colonialism is often used interchangeably with imperialism, the latter is sometimes used more broadly as it covers control excercized informally (via influence) as well as formal military control or economic leverage.
Imperialism	Imperialism is the policy of extending a nation's authority by territorial acquisition or by the establishment of economic and political hegemony over other nations, countries, or colonies. This is realized either through direct territorial conquest or settlement, or through indirect methods of influencing or controlling the politics and/or economy.
Status quo	Status quo is a Latin termpresent, current, existing state of affairs. To maintain the status quo is to keep the things the way they presently are. The related phrase status quo ante, means "the state of things as it was before."
Free Press	Free Press is a non-partisan, non-profit organization founded by media critic Robert McChesney to promote more democratic media policy in the United States.

Go to **Cram101.com** for the Practice Tests for this Chapter.

International relations	International relations a branch of political science, is the study of foreign relations and global issues among states within the international system, including the roles of states, inter-governmental organizations, non-governmental organizations, and multinational corporations. It is both an academic and public policy field, and can be either positive or normative as it both seeks to analyze as well as formulate the foreign policy of particular states.
Sovereignty	Sovereignty is the exclusive right to exercise supreme political authority over a geographic region, group of people, or oneself. The source or justification of sovereignty ("by God" or "by people") must be distinguished from its exercise by branches of government. In democratic states, sovereignty is held by the people.
Legitimacy	Legitimacy in political science, is the popular acceptance of a governing regime or law as an authority. Where as authority refers to a specific position in an established government, the term legitimacy is used when describing a system of government itself —where "government may be generalized to mean the wider "sphere of influence."
Republic	A republic is a form of government maintained by a state or country whose sovereignty is based on popular consent and whose governance is based on popular representation and control. Several definitions stress the importance of the rule of law as among the requirements for a republic.
Representation	In politics, representation describes how residents of a country are empowered in the government. Representation usually refers to representative democracies, where elected representatives speak for their constituents in the legislature. Generally, only citizens are granted representation in the government in the form of voting rights, however some democracies have extended this right further.
Anarchism	Anarchism is a political philosophy or group of doctrines and attitudes centered on rejection of any form of compulsory government and supporting its elimination. Thus anarchism, in its most general meaning, is the belief that all forms of rulership and thus also involuntary servitude are undesirable and should be abolished.
Reasons of state	The reasons of state is a country's goals and ambitions whether economic, military, or cultural. The notion is an important one in international relations where pursuit of the national interest is the foundation of the realist school.
Ideology	An ideology is an organized collection of ideas. The word ideology was coined by Count Antoine Destutt de Tracy in the late 18th century to define a "science of ideas." An ideology can be thought of as a comprehensive vision, as a way of looking at things, as in common sense and several philosophical tendencies, or a set of ideas proposed by the dominant class of a society to all members of this society.
Communism	Communism is an ideology that seeks to establish a classless, stateless social organization based on common ownership of the means of production. It can be considered a branch of the broader socialist movement. Communism as a political goal is generally a conjectured form of future social organization, although Marxists have described early forms of human social organization as 'primitive communism'.
Capitalism	Capitalism generally refers to an economic system in which the means of production are mostly privately owned and operated for profit, and in which distribution, production and pricing of goods and services are determined in a largely free market. It is usually considered to involve the right of individuals and groups of individuals acting as "legal persons" or corporations to trade capital goods, labor, land and money.
Foreign policy	A country's foreign policy is a set of political goals that seeks to outline how that particular country will interact with other countries of the world and, to a lesser extent, non-state actors. They generally are designed to help protect a country's national

Go to **Cram101.com** for the Practice Tests for this Chapter.

interests, national security, ideological goals, and economic prosperity.

Currency	A currency is a unit of exchange, facilitating the transfer of goods and services. It is a form of money, where money is an efficient medium of exchange, and it is also considered by several people as a store of value, created through a claim to its central bank assets.
Geopolitics	**Geopolitics** is the study that analyzes geography, history and social science with reference to spatial politics and patterns at various scales. It examines the political, economic and strategic significance of geography, where geography is defined in terms of the location, size, function, and relationships of places and resources.
Industrializ-tion	Industrialisation (also spelt **Industrialization**) or an Industrial Revolution is a process of social and economic change whereby a human society is transformed from a pre-industrial to an industrial state.
Peacekeeping	Peacekeeping, as defined by the United Nations, is "a way to help countries torn by conflict create conditions for sustainable peace.
Authoritarianism	Authoritarianism describes a form of social control characterized by strict obedience to the authority of a state or organization, often maintaining and enforcing control through the use of oppressive measures.
Coalition	A coalition is an alliance among entities, during which they cooperate in joint action, each in their own self-interest. This alliance may be temporary or a matter of convenience. A coalition government, in a parliamentary system, is a government composed of a coalition of parties.
Regime	A regime is the set of rules, both formal and informal that regulate the operation of government and its interactions with the economy and society.
Initiative	In political science, the initiative provides a means by which a petition signed by a certain minimum number of registered voters can force a public vote on a proposed statute, constitutional amendment, charter amendment or ordinance, or, in its minimal form, to simply oblige the executive or legislative bodies to consider the subject by submitting it to the order of the day.
Diplomacy	Diplomacy is the art and practice of conducting negotiations between representatives of groups or states. It usually refers to international diplomacy, the conduct of international relations through the intercession of professional diplomats with regard to issues of peace-making, trade, war, economics and culture. International treaties are usually negotiated by diplomats prior to endorsement by national politicians.
Deterrence	Deterrence theory is a military strategy developed after and used throughout the Cold War and current times. It is especially relevant with regard to the use of nuclear weapons, and figures prominently on current United States foreign policy regarding the development of nuclear technology in North Korea and Iran.
Diplomatic recognition	Diplomatic recognition is a political act by which one state acknowledges an act or status of another state or government, thereby according it legitimacy and expressing its intent to bring into force the domestic and international legal consequences of recognition.
Reciprocity	In international relations and treaties, the principle of reciprocity states that favours, benefits, or penalties that are granted by one state to the citizens or legal entities of another, should be returned in kind.
Constituency	The most common meaning of constituency occurs in politics and means either the group of people from whom an individual or organization hopes to attract support, or the group of people or geographical area that a particular elected representative or group of elected representatives represents.

Go to **Cram101.com** for the Practice Tests for this Chapter.

Trade organization	Trade organization is generally a public relations organization founded and funded by corporations that operate in a specific industry. Its purpose is generally to promote the industry through PR activities such as advertizing, education, political donations, lobbying and publishing.
World Trade Organization	World Trade Organization is an international organization designed to supervise and liberalize international trade. The WTO came into being on January 1, 1995, and is the successor to the General Agreement on Tariffs and Trade, which was created in 1947, and continued to operate for almost five decades as a de facto international organization.
Balance of trade	Balance of trade is the difference between the monetary value of exports and imports in an economy over a certain period of time.
Economism	Economism is a term used to criticize economic reductionism, that is the reduction of all social facts to economical dimensions. It is also used to criticize economics as an ideology, in which supply and demand are the only important factors in decisions, and literally outstrip or permit ignoring all other factors.
New International Economic Order	The New International Economic Order (NIEO) was a set of proposals put forward during the 1970s by developing countries through the United Nations Conference on Trade and Development to promote their interests by improving their terms of trade, increasing development assistance, developed-country tariff reductions, and other means.
Humanitarianism	Humanitarianism is an informal ideology of practice, whereby people practice humane treatment and provide assistance to others.
Democracy	Democracy is a form of government in which supreme power is vested in the people and exercised by them directly or indirectly through a system of representation usually involving periodic free elections.
Human rights	Human rights refers to universal rights of people regardless of jurisdiction or other factors, such as ethnicity, age, nationality, sexual orientation or religion.
Boycott	A boycott is the act of abstaining from using, buying, or dealing with someone or some other organization as an expression of protest or as a means of coercion.
Hegemony	Hegemony is the dominance of one group over other groups, with or without the threat of force, to the extent that, for instance, the dominant party can dictate the terms of trade to its advantage; more broadly, cultural perspectives become skewed to favor the dominant group. The cultural control that hegemony asserts affects commonplace patterns of thought: hegemony controls the way new ideas are rejected or become naturalized in a process that subtly alters notions of common sense in a given society.
Litigation	A lawsuit, also known as litigation, is a criminal or civil action brought before a court in which the party commencing the action, the plaintiff, seeks a legal remedy. Often, one or more defendants are required to answer the plaintiff's complaint.
Tariff	A tariff is a tax on foreign goods upon importation. When a ship arrives in port a customs officer inspects the contents and charges a tax according to the tariff formula. Since the goods cannot be landed until the tax is paid it is the easiest tax to collect, and the cost of collection is small. Smugglers of course seek to evade the tariff.
Apartheid	Apartheid was a system of racial segregation that was enforced in South Africa from 1948, and was dismantled in a series of negotiations from 1990 to 1993, culminating in democratic elections in 1994. Apartheid was designed to form a legal framework for continued economic and political dominance by people of European descent.
United Nations	The United Nations is an international organization whose stated aims are to facilitate co-operation in international law, international security, economic development, social progress

Go to **Cram101.com** for the Practice Tests for this Chapter.
And, **NEVER** highlight a book again!

	and human rights issues.
Economic sanction	A economic sanction is a economic penalty applied by one country on another for a variety of reasons. They include, but are not limited to, tariffs, trade barriers, import duties, and import or export quotas.
Unitary State	A Unitary State is a state or country that is governed constitutionally as one single unit, with one constitutionally created legislature. The political power of government in such states may well be transferred to lower levels, to regionally or locally elected assemblies, governors and mayors, but the central government retains the principal right to recall such delegated power.
National security	National security refers to the requirement to maintain the survival of the nation-state through the use of economic, military and political power and the exercise of diplomacy.
Cold War	The Cold War was the period of conflict, tension and competition between the United States and the Soviet Union and their respective allies from the mid-1940s until the early 1990s.
Standard operating procedure	The standard operating procedure is used in a variety of different contexts, from everyday use , to industry and the military.
Bureaucracy	Bureaucracy is a concept in sociology and political science referring to the way that the administrative execution and enforcement of legal rules are socially organized. This office organization is characterized by standardized procedure, formal division of responsibility, hierarchy, and impersonal relationships.
Cloture	Cloture is a motion or process aimed at bringing debate to a quick end. The procedure originated in the French National Assembly, from which the name in French is taken. It was introduced into the United Kingdom Parliament by William Gladstone to overcome the obstruction of the Irish nationalist party and was made permanent in 1887. It was subsequently adopted by the United States Senate and other legislatures.
Constituent	A constituent is someone who can or does appoint or elect another as their agent or representative.
Interest group	An interest group is a group, however loosely or tightly organized, doing advocacy: those determined to encourage or prevent changes in public policy without trying to be elected.
Corporation	A corporation is an artificial legal entity which, while made up of a number of natural persons or other legal entities, has a separate legal identity from them. As a legal entity the corporation receives legal rights and duties
Multinational corporation	A multinational corporation is a corporation or enterprise that manages production establishments or delivers services in at least two countries. Very large multinationals have budgets that exceed those of many countries. They can have a powerful influence in international relations and local economies.
Globalization	Globalization is an umbrella term and is perhaps best understood as a unitary process inclusive of many sub-processes (such as enhanced economic interdependence, increased cultural influence, rapid advances of information technology, and novel governance and geopolitical challenges) that are increasingly binding people and the biosphere more tightly into one global system.
Islamism	Islamism is a term used to denote a set of political ideologies holding that Islam is not solely a religion, but also a political system. Islamism holds that Islamic law (sharia) must be the basis for all statutory law of society; that Muslims must return to the original teachings and the early models of Islam; and that western military, economic, political, social, or cultural influence on the Muslim world is against Islam.

Go to **Cram101.com** for the Practice Tests for this Chapter.

Fundamentalism	**Fundamentalism** originally referred to a movement in North American Protestantism that arose in the early part of the 20th century in reaction to modernism (see below, "History"), stressing that the Bible is literally inerrant, not only in matters of faith and morals but also as a literal historical record.
Liberal democracy	Liberal democracy is a form of government. It is a representative democracy in which the ability of the elected representatives to exercise decision-making power is subject to the rule of law, and usually moderated by a constitution that emphasizes the protection of the rights and freedoms of individuals, and which places constraints on the leaders and on the extent to which the will of the majority can be exercized against the rights of minorities.
Terrorism	As a form of unconventional warfare, terrorism is sometimes used when attempting to force political change by: convincing a government or population to agree to demands to avoid future harm or fear of harm, destabilization of an existing government, motivating a disgruntled population to join an uprizing, escalating a conflict in the hopes of disrupting the status quo, expressing a grievance, or drawing attention to a cause.
Collective action	Collective action is the pursuit of a goal or set of goals by more than one person. It is a term which has formulations and theories in many areas of the social sciences.
Autonomy	Autonomy means freedom from external authority. In politics, autonomy refers to self-governance.
Interdependence	Interdependence is a dynamic of being mutually responsible to and sharing a common set of principles with others. This concept differs distinctly from "dependence" in that an interdependent relationship implies that all participants are emotionally, economically, and/or morally "independent." Some people advocate freedom or independence as a sort of ultimate good; others do the same with devotion to one's family, community, or society. Interdependence recognizes the truth in each position and weaves them together.
Lobbying	Lobbying is a concerted effort designed to achieve some result, typically from government authorities and elected officials. It can consist of the private cajoling of legislative members, public actions, or combinations of both public and private actions.
Democratization	Democratization is the transition from an authoritarian or a semi-authoritarian political system to a democratic political system. There is considerable debate about the factors which affect or ultimately limit democratization. A great many things, including economics, culture, and history, have been cited as impacting on the process.

Go to **Cram101.com** for the Practice Tests for this Chapter.

International relations	International relations a branch of political science, is the study of foreign relations and global issues among states within the international system, including the roles of states, inter-governmental organizations, non-governmental organizations, and multinational corporations. It is both an academic and public policy field, and can be either positive or normative as it both seeks to analyze as well as formulate the foreign policy of particular states.
Foreign policy	A country's foreign policy is a set of political goals that seeks to outline how that particular country will interact with other countries of the world and, to a lesser extent, non-state actors. They generally are designed to help protect a country's national interests, national security, ideological goals, and economic prosperity.
Corporation	A corporation is an artificial legal entity which, while made up of a number of natural persons or other legal entities, has a separate legal identity from them. As a legal entity the corporation receives legal rights and duties
Multinational corporation	A multinational corporation is a corporation or enterprise that manages production establishments or delivers services in at least two countries. Very large multinationals have budgets that exceed those of many countries. They can have a powerful influence in international relations and local economies.
Political economy	Political economy was the original term for the study of production, the acts of buying and selling, and their relationships to laws, customs and government. It developed in the 18th century as the study of the economies of states.
Communist Party	In modern usage, the term communist party is generally used to identify any political party which has adopted communist ideology. However, the Leninist concept of a communist party includes not only ideological orientation, but also a wide set of organizational policies.
Warsaw Pact	The Warsaw Pact was an organization of Central and Eastern European communist states. It was prompted by the integration of a " re-militarized" West Germany into NATO via ratification of the Paris Peace Treaties. It lasted throughout the Cold War.
Glasnost	**Glasnost** is a Russian word for "transparency" or "openness." Mikhail Gorbachev used the term to describe a program of reform introduced to the Soviet Union in 1985 whose goals included combating corruption and the abuse of privilege by the political classes.
Perestroika	**Perestroika** , is the Russian term for the economic reforms introduced in June 1985 by the Soviet leader Mikhail Gorbachev. Its literal meaning is "restructuring", referring to the restructuring of the Soviet economy.
Republic	A republic is a form of government maintained by a state or country whose sovereignty is based on popular consent and whose governance is based on popular representation and control. Several definitions stress the importance of the rule of law as among the requirements for a republic.
Democracy	Democracy is a form of government in which supreme power is vested in the people and exercised by them directly or indirectly through a system of representation usually involving periodic free elections.
Standard operating procedure	The standard operating procedure is used in a variety of different contexts, from everyday use , to industry and the military.
Cuban Missile Crisis	The Cuban Missile Crisis was a confrontation during the Cold War between the Government of the United States, the Government of the Soviet Union, and the Government of Cuba. This crisis is generally regarded as the moment when the Cold War came closest to escalating into a nuclear war.

Go to **Cram101.com** for the Practice Tests for this Chapter.

45

Nationalism	Nationalism, in its broadest sense, is a devotion to one's own nation and its interests over those of all other nations. The term can also refer to a doctrine or political movement that holds that a nation—usually defined in terms of ethnicity or culture—has the right to constitute an independent or autonomous political community based on a shared history and common destiny.
United Nations	The United Nations is an international organization whose stated aims are to facilitate co-operation in international law, international security, economic development, social progress and human rights issues.
Totalitarianism	Totalitarianism is a term employed by political scientists, especially those in the field of comparative politics, to describe modern regimes in which the state regulates nearly every aspect of public and private behavior.
Communism	Communism is an ideology that seeks to establish a classless, stateless social organization based on common ownership of the means of production. It can be considered a branch of the broader socialist movement. Communism as a political goal is generally a conjectured form of future social organization, although Marxists have described early forms of human social organization as 'primitive communism'.
Prime minister	A prime minister is the most senior minister of a cabinet in the executive branch of government in a parliamentary system.
Cold War	The Cold War was the period of conflict, tension and competition between the United States and the Soviet Union and their respective allies from the mid-1940s until the early 1990s.
Ethnic cleansing	Ethnic cleansing refers to various policies or practices aimed at the displacement of an ethnic group from a particular territory in order to create ethnically pure society. The term entered English and international usage in the early 1990s to describe certain events in the former Yugoslavia. Its typical usage was developed in the Balkans, to be a less objectionable code-word meaning "genocide", but its intent was to best avoid the obvious pitfalls of longstanding international treaty laws prohibiting war-crimes.
Diplomacy	Diplomacy is the art and practice of conducting negotiations between representatives of groups or states. It usually refers to international diplomacy, the conduct of international relations through the intercession of professional diplomats with regard to issues of peace-making, trade, war, economics and culture. International treaties are usually negotiated by diplomats prior to endorsement by national politicians.
Declaration of Independence	The United States Declaration of Independence was an act of the Second Continental Congress, adopted on July 4, 1776, which declared that the Thirteen Colonies were independent of the Kingdom of Florida.
Family law	Family law is an area of the law that deals with family-related issues and domestic relations. In many jurisdictions in the United States, the family courts see the most crowded dockets. Litigants representative of all social and economic classes are parties within the system.
Democratization	Democratization is the transition from an authoritarian or a semi-authoritarian political system to a democratic political system. There is considerable debate about the factors which affect or ultimately limit democratization. A great many things, including economics, culture, and history, have been cited as impacting on the process.
Initiative	In political science, the initiative provides a means by which a petition signed by a certain minimum number of registered voters can force a public vote on a proposed statute, constitutional amendment, charter amendment or ordinance, or, in its minimal form, to simply oblige the executive or legislative bodies to consider the subject by submitting it to the order of the day.

Division of labor	Division of labor is the specialisation of cooperative labor in specific, circumscribed tasks and roles, intended to increase efficiency of output. Historically the growth of a more and more complex division of labor is closely associated with the growth of trade, the rise of capitalism, and of the complexity of industrialisation processes.
Authoritarianism	Authoritarianism describes a form of social control characterized by strict obedience to the authority of a state or organization, often maintaining and enforcing control through the use of oppressive measures.
Legitimacy	Legitimacy in political science, is the popular acceptance of a governing regime or law as an authority. Where as authority refers to a specific position in an established government, the term legitimacy is used when describing a system of government itself —where "government may be generalized to mean the wider "sphere of influence."
Treaty	A treaty is an agreement under international law entered into by actors in international law, namely states and international organizations. Under United States constitutional law, only a treaty that has achieved advice and consent of two-thirds of the Senate present is properly designated as a treaty.
Referendum	A referendum is a direct vote in which an entire electorate is asked to either accept or reject a particular proposal. This may be the adoption of a new constitution, a constitutional amendment, a law, the recall of an elected official or simply a specific government policy. The referendum is a form of direct democracy.
Opinion poll	An opinion poll is a survey of opinion from a particular sample. They are usually designed to represent the opinions of a population by asking a small number of people a series of questions and then extrapolating the answers to the larger group within confidence intervals.
Free trade	Free trade is a market model in which trade in goods and services between or within countries flows unhindered by government-imposed restrictions. Restrictions to trade include taxes and other legislation, such as tariff and non-tariff trade barriers.
Protectionism	Protectionism is the economic policy of restraining trade between nations, through methods such as high tariffs on imported goods, restrictive quotas, a variety of restrictive government regulations designed to discourage imports, and anti-dumping laws in an attempt to protect domestic industries in a particular nation from foreign take-over or competition.
Humanitarianism	Humanitarianism is an informal ideology of practice, whereby people practice humane treatment and provide assistance to others.
Welfare	Welfare is financial assistance paid by taxpayers to groups of people who are unable to support themselves, and determined to be able to function more effectively with financial assistance.
Regime	A regime is the set of rules, both formal and informal that regulate the operation of government and its interactions with the economy and society.
Reasons of state	The reasons of state is a country's goals and ambitions whether economic, military, or cultural. The notion is an important one in international relations where pursuit of the national interest is the foundation of the realist school.
National security	National security refers to the requirement to maintain the survival of the nation-state through the use of economic, military and political power and the exercise of diplomacy.
Isolationism	Isolationism is a foreign policy which combines a non-interventionist military policy and a political policy of economic nationalism (protectionism). Non-interventionism - Political rulers should avoid entangling alliances with other nations and avoid all wars not related to direct territorial self-defense. Protectionism - There should be legal barriers to prevent trade and cultural exchange with people in other states.

Go to **Cram101.com** for the Practice Tests for this Chapter.

Security dilemma	In international relations, the security dilemma refers to a situation wherein two or more states are drawn into conflict, possibly even war, over security concerns, even though none of the states actually desire conflict.
Peacekeeping	Peacekeeping, as defined by the United Nations, is "a way to help countries torn by conflict create conditions for sustainable peace.
International relations	International relations a branch of political science, is the study of foreign relations and global issues among states within the international system, including the roles of states, inter-governmental organizations, non-governmental organizations, and multinational corporations. It is both an academic and public policy field, and can be either positive or normative as it both seeks to analyze as well as formulate the foreign policy of particular states.
Collective security	Collective Security is a system aspiring to the maintenance of peace, in which participants agree that any "breach of the peace is to be declared to be of concern to all the participating states," 1 and will result in a collective response. This began in 1918 after the international balance of power was perceived by many nations to be no longer working correctly.
Arms control	Arms control is an umbrella term for restrictions upon the development, production, stockpiling, proliferation, and usage of weapons, especially weapons of mass destruction. Arms control is typically exercised through the use of diplomacy which seeks to impose such limitations upon consenting participants through international treaties and agreements, although it may also comprise efforts by a nation or group of nations to enforce limitations upon a non-consenting country.
Disarmament	**Disarmament** means the act of reducing or depriving arms i.e. weaponry. Disarmament can be contrasted with "arms control," which essentially refers to the act of "controlling arms," rather than eliminating them.
Balance of power	Balance of power refers to the division, distribution, or separation of powers within a national political system.
Deterrence	Deterrence theory is a military strategy developed after and used throughout the Cold War and current times. It is especially relevant with regard to the use of nuclear weapons, and figures prominently on current United States foreign policy regarding the development of nuclear technology in North Korea and Iran.
Veto	Veto is used to denote that a certain party has the right to stop unilaterally a certain piece of legislation. A veto gives power, possibly unlimited, to stop changes, but not to adopt them.
North Atlantic Treaty Organization	The North Atlantic Treaty Organization is a military alliance, the strongest in the world, established by the signing of the North Atlantic Treaty on April 4, 1949. With headquarters in Brussels, Belgium, the organisation established a system of collective defense whereby its member states agree to mutual defense in response to an attack by any external party, and promote liberty around the world.
Treaty	A treaty is an agreement under international law entered into by actors in international law, namely states and international organizations. Under United States constitutional law, only a treaty that has achieved advice and consent of two-thirds of the Senate present is properly designated as a treaty.
Status quo	Status quo is a Latin termpresent, current, existing state of affairs. To maintain the status quo is to keep the things the way they presently are. The related phrase status quo ante, means "the state of things as it was before."
Cold War	The Cold War was the period of conflict, tension and competition between the United States

Go to **Cram101.com** for the Practice Tests for this Chapter.

and the Soviet Union and their respective allies from the mid-1940s until the early 1990s.

United Nations	The United Nations is an international organization whose stated aims are to facilitate co-operation in international law, international security, economic development, social progress and human rights issues.
Cuban Missile Crisis	The Cuban Missile Crisis was a confrontation during the Cold War between the Government of the United States, the Government of the Soviet Union, and the Government of Cuba. This crisis is generally regarded as the moment when the Cold War came closest to escalating into a nuclear war.
Bilateral	**Bilateral**ism is a term referring to political and cultural relations between two states. Most international diplomacy is done bilaterally. Examples of this include treaties between two countries, exchanges of ambassadors, and state visits. The alternatives to bilateral relations are multilateral relations, which involve many states, and unilateralism, when one state acts on its own.
Nuclear proliferation	Nuclear proliferation is a term now used to describe the spread of nuclear weapons, fissile material, and weapons-applicable nuclear technology and information, to nations which are not recognized as "nuclear weapon States" by the Treaty on the Nonproliferation of Nuclear Weapons
Warsaw Pact	The Warsaw Pact was an organization of Central and Eastern European communist states. It was prompted by the integration of a " re-militarized" West Germany into NATO via ratification of the Paris Peace Treaties. It lasted throughout the Cold War.
Regime	A regime is the set of rules, both formal and informal that regulate the operation of government and its interactions with the economy and society.
Constituency	The most common meaning of constituency occurs in politics and means either the group of people from whom an individual or organization hopes to attract support, or the group of people or geographical area that a particular elected representative or group of elected representatives represents.
Republic	A republic is a form of government maintained by a state or country whose sovereignty is based on popular consent and whose governance is based on popular representation and control. Several definitions stress the importance of the rule of law as among the requirements for a republic.
Superpower	A superpower is a state with a leading position in the international system and the ability to influence events and project power on a worldwide scale; it is considered a higher level of power than a great power.
Mandate	In international law, a mandate is a binding obligation issued from an inter-governmental organization like the United Nations to a country which is bound to follow the instructions of the organization.
Human rights	Human rights refers to universal rights of people regardless of jurisdiction or other factors, such as ethnicity, age, nationality, sexual orientation or religion.
Law and order	In politics, law and order refers to a political platform which supports a strict criminal justice system, especially in relation to violent crime and property crime, through harsher criminal penalties. These penalties may include longer terms of imprisonment, mandatory sentencing, and in some countries, capital punishment.
Humanitarianism	Humanitarianism is an informal ideology of practice, whereby people practice humane treatment and provide assistance to others.
Human nature	Human nature is the fundamental nature and substance of humans, as well as the range of human behavior that is, believed to be invariant over long periods of time and across very

different cultural contexts.

Reprieve	Reprieve is the name of a number of not-for-profit organizations around the world which work against the death penalty, with a particular focus on legal support for those facing the death penalty.
Representative government	Representative government is a form of government founded on the principles of popular sovereignty by the people's representatives. The representatives are charged with the responsibility of acting in the people's interest, but not as their proxy representative.
Separation of powers	Separation of powers, a term coined by French political Enlightenment thinker Baron de Montesquieu, is a model for the governance of democratic states. Under this model the state is divided into branches, and each branch of the state has separate and independent powers and areas of responsibility. The normal division of branches is into the Executive, the Legislative, and the Judicial.
Democracy	Democracy is a form of government in which supreme power is vested in the people and exercised by them directly or indirectly through a system of representation usually involving periodic free elections.
Inflation	In mainstream economics, the word inflation refers to a general rise in prices measured against a standard level of purchasing power. Previously the term was used to refer to an increase in the money supply, which is now referred to as expansionary monetary policy or monetary inflation.
Capitalism	Capitalism generally refers to an economic system in which the means of production are mostly privately owned and operated for profit, and in which distribution, production and pricing of goods and services are determined in a largely free market. It is usually considered to involve the right of individuals and groups of individuals acting as "legal persons" or corporations to trade capital goods, labor, land and money.
Proletariat	The **proletariat** is a term used to identify a lower social class; a member of such a class is proletarian. Originally it was identified as those people who had no wealth other than their sons; the term was initially used in a derogatory sense, until Karl Marx used it as a sociological term to refer to the working class.
Economic Growth	Economic growth is the increase in value of the goods and services produced by an economy. It is conventionally measured as the percent rate of increase in real gross domestic product, or GDP. Growth is usually calculated in real terms, i.e. inflation-adjusted terms, in order to net out the effect of inflation on the price of the goods and services produced.
Economism	Economism is a term used to criticize economic reductionism, that is the reduction of all social facts to economical dimensions. It is also used to criticize economics as an ideology, in which supply and demand are the only important factors in decisions, and literally outstrip or permit ignoring all other factors.
Colonialism	Colonialism is the extension of a nation's sovereignty over territory beyond its borders by the establishment of either settler colonies or administrative dependencies in which indigenous populations are directly ruled or displaced. Colonizing nations generally dominate the resources, labor, and markets of the colonial territory, and may also impose socio-cultural, religious and linguistic structures on the conquered population (see also cultural imperialism). Though the word colonialism is often used interchangeably with imperialism, the latter is sometimes used more broadly as it covers control exercised informally (via influence) as well as formal military control or economic leverage.
Imperialism	Imperialism is the policy of extending a nation's authority by territorial acquisition or by the establishment of economic and political hegemony over other nations, countries, or colonies. This is realized either through direct territorial conquest or settlement, or

Go to **Cram101.com** for the Practice Tests for this Chapter.

55

through indirect methods of influencing or controlling the politics and/or economy.

Rule of law	The rule of law is the principle that governmental authority is legitimately exercized only in accordance with written, publicly disclosed laws adopted and enforced in accordance with established procedure.
Sovereignty	Sovereignty is the exclusive right to exercise supreme political authority over a geographic region, group of people, or oneself. The source or justification of sovereignty ("by God" or "by people") must be distinguished from its exercise by branches of government. In democratic states, sovereignty is held by the people.
Anarchism	Anarchism is a political philosophy or group of doctrines and attitudes centered on rejection of any form of compulsory government and supporting its elimination. Thus anarchism, in its most general meaning, is the belief that all forms of rulership and thus also involuntary servitude are undesirable and should be abolished.
Communist Party	In modern usage, the term communist party is generally used to identify any political party which has adopted communist ideology. However, the Leninist concept of a communist party includes not only ideological orientation, but also a wide set of organizational policies.
Nationalism	Nationalism, in its broadest sense, is a devotion to one's own nation and its interests over those of all other nations. The term can also refer to a doctrine or political movement that holds that a nation—usually defined in terms of ethnicity or culture—has the right to constitute an independent or autonomous political community based on a shared history and common destiny.
Economic sanction	A economic sanction is a economic penalty applied by one country on another for a variety of reasons. They include, but are not limited to, tariffs, trade barriers, import duties, and import or export quotas.
Terrorism	As a form of unconventional warfare, terrorism is sometimes used when attempting to force political change by: convincing a government or population to agree to demands to avoid future harm or fear of harm, destabilization of an existing government, motivating a disgruntled population to join an uprizing, escalating a conflict in the hopes of disrupting the status quo, expressing a grievance, or drawing attention to a cause.
Third party	In any two-party system of politics, a third party is a party other than the two dominant ones. While technically the term is limited to the third largest party, it is often used as (innumerate) shorthand to describe any smaller party.
Fundamentalism	**Fundamentalism** originally referred to a movement in North American Protestantism that arose in the early part of the 20th century in reaction to modernism (see below, "History"), stressing that the Bible is literally inerrant, not only in matters of faith and morals but also as a literal historical record.
Muslim	A Muslim is an adherent of the religion of Islam. The feminine form of Muslim is Muslimah. Literally, the word means "one who submits to God. They believe that there is only one God, translated to Arabic as Allah.
Legislation	Legislation is law which has been promulgated (or "enacted") by a legislature or other governing body. The term may refer to a single law, or the collective body of enacted law, while "statute" is also used to refer to a single law. Before an item of legislation becomes law it may be known as a bill, which is typically also known as "legislation" while it remains under active consideration.
National security	National security refers to the requirement to maintain the survival of the nation-state through the use of economic, military and political power and the exercise of diplomacy.
Civil rights	Civil rights are the protections and privileges of personal power given to all citizens by

	law. Civil rights are distinguished from "human rights" or "natural rights", also called "our God-given rights". They are rights that are bestowed by nations on those within their territorial boundaries, while natural or human rights are rights that many scholars claim should belong to all people.
Internationalism	Internationalism is a political movement which advocates a greater economic and political cooperation among nations for the benefit of all. Partisans of this movement, such as supporters of the World Federalist Movement, claim that nations should cooperate because their long-term mutual interests are of greater value than their individual short-term needs.
Foreign policy	A country's foreign policy is a set of political goals that seeks to outline how that particular country will interact with other countries of the world and, to a lesser extent, non-state actors. They generally are designed to help protect a country's national interests, national security, ideological goals, and economic prosperity.

Political economy	Political economy was the original term for the study of production, the acts of buying and selling, and their relationships to laws, customs and government. It developed in the 18th century as the study of the economies of states.
Globalization	Globalization is an umbrella term and is perhaps best understood as a unitary process inclusive of many sub-processes (such as enhanced economic interdependence, increased cultural influence, rapid advances of information technology, and novel governance and geopolitical challenges) that are increasingly binding people and the biosphere more tightly into one global system.
Economism	Economism is a term used to criticize economic reductionism, that is the reduction of all social facts to economical dimensions. It is also used to criticize economics as an ideology, in which supply and demand are the only important factors in decisions, and literally outstrip or permit ignoring all other factors.
New International Economic Order	The New International Economic Order (NIEO) was a set of proposals put forward during the 1970s by developing countries through the United Nations Conference on Trade and Development to promote their interests by improving their terms of trade, increasing development assistance, developed-country tariff reductions, and other means.
Free trade	Free trade is a market model in which trade in goods and services between or within countries flows unhindered by government-imposed restrictions. Restrictions to trade include taxes and other legislation, such as tariff and non-tariff trade barriers.
North American Free Trade Agreement	The North American Free Trade Area is the trade bloc in North America created by the North American Free Trade Agreement and its two supplements, the North American Agreement on Environmental Cooperation and The North American Agreement on Labor Cooperation, whose members are Canada, Mexico and the United States. It came into effect on 1 January 1994.
Corporation	A corporation is an artificial legal entity which, while made up of a number of natural persons or other legal entities, has a separate legal identity from them. As a legal entity the corporation receives legal rights and duties
Multinational corporation	A multinational corporation is a corporation or enterprise that manages production establishments or delivers services in at least two countries. Very large multinationals have budgets that exceed those of many countries. They can have a powerful influence in international relations and local economies.
International relations	International relations a branch of political science, is the study of foreign relations and global issues among states within the international system, including the roles of states, inter-governmental organizations, non-governmental organizations, and multinational corporations. It is both an academic and public policy field, and can be either positive or normative as it both seeks to analyze as well as formulate the foreign policy of particular states.
World Bank	The World Bank Group is a group of five international organizations responsible for providing finance and advice to countries for the purposes of economic development and eliminating poverty.
International Monetary Fund	The International Monetary Fund is an international organization that oversees the global financial system by observing exchange rates and balance of payments, as well as offering financial and technical assistance. Its headquarters are located in Washington, D.C., USA.
Statism	Statism is a term that is used to describe specific instances of state intervention in personal, social or economic matters. A form of government or economic system that involves significant state intervention in personal, social, or economic matters.
Radicalism	Radicalism is a political movement for those favouring or trying to produce thoroughgoing political reforms which can include changes to the social order to a greater or lesser extent

	toward the right.
Mercantilism	Mercantilism is an economic theory that holds that the prosperity of a nation depends upon its supply of capital, and that the global volume of trade is "unchangeable". Economic assets, or Capital, are represented by bullion (gold, silver, and trade value) held by the state, which is best increased through a positive balance of trade with other nations (exports minus imports). Mercantilism suggests that the ruling government should advance these goals by playing a protectionist role in the economy, by encouraging exports and discouraging imports, especially through the use of tariffs. The economic policy based upon these ideas is often called the mercantile system.
Marxism	Marxism of Karl Marx and Friedrich Engels. Any political practice or theory that is based on an interpretation of the works of Marx and Engels may be termed Marxism.
Human nature	Human nature is the fundamental nature and substance of humans, as well as the range of human behavior that is, believed to be invariant over long periods of time and across very different cultural contexts.
Redistricting	Redistricting is the changing of political borders. Often this means changing electoral district and constituency boundaries, usually in response to periodic census results. This takes place by law or constitution at least every decade in most representative democracy systems using first-past-the-post or similar electoral systems to prevent geographic malapportionment.
Industrializ-tion	Industrialisation (also spelt **Industrialization**) or an Industrial Revolution is a process of social and economic change whereby a human society is transformed from a pre-industrial to an industrial state.
Balance of payments	Balance of payments measures the payments that flow between any individual country and all other countries. It is used to summarize all international economic transactions for that country during a specific time period, usually a year. The Balance of payments is determined by the country's exports and imports of goods, services, and financial capital, as well as financial transfers. It reflects all payments and liabilities to foreigners (debits) and all payments and obligations received from foreigners (credits).
Reasons of state	The reasons of state is a country's goals and ambitions whether economic, military, or cultural. The notion is an important one in international relations where pursuit of the national interest is the foundation of the realist school.
Economic policy	Economic policy refers to the actions that governments take in the economic field. It covers the systems for setting interest rates and government deficit as well as the labor market, national ownership, and many other areas of government.
Anarchism	Anarchism is a political philosophy or group of doctrines and attitudes centered on rejection of any form of compulsory government and supporting its elimination. Thus anarchism, in its most general meaning, is the belief that all forms of rulership and thus also involuntary servitude are undesirable and should be abolished.
Security dilemma	In international relations, the security dilemma refers to a situation wherein two or more states are drawn into conflict, possibly even war, over security concerns, even though none of the states actually desire conflict.
Welfare	Welfare is financial assistance paid by taxpayers to groups of people who are unable to support themselves, and determined to be able to function more effectively with financial assistance.
Comparative advantage	In economics, the theory of comparative advantage explains why it can be beneficial for two parties (countries, regions, individuals and so on) to trade if one has a lower relative cost of producing some good. What matters is not the absolute cost of production but the

opportunity cost, which measures how much production of one good is reduced to produce one more unit of the other good. Comparative advantage is critical to understanding modern international trade theory.

Interdependence	Interdependence is a dynamic of being mutually responsible to and sharing a common set of principles with others. This concept differs distinctly from "dependence" in that an interdependent relationship implies that all participants are emotionally, economically, and/or morally "independent." Some people advocate freedom or independence as a sort of ultimate good; others do the same with devotion to one's family, community, or society. Interdependence recognizes the truth in each position and weaves them together.
Socialism	Socialism refers to a broad array of doctrines or political movements that envisage a socio-economic system in which property and the distribution of wealth are subject to control by the community.
Communism	Communism is an ideology that seeks to establish a classless, stateless social organization based on common ownership of the means of production. It can be considered a branch of the broader socialist movement. Communism as a political goal is generally a conjectured form of future social organization, although Marxists have described early forms of human social organization as 'primitive communism'.
Political Party	A political party is a political organization that seeks to attain political power within a government, usually by participating in electoral campaigns. They often espouse a certain ideology and vision, but may also represent a coalition among disparate interests.
Cold War	The Cold War was the period of conflict, tension and competition between the United States and the Soviet Union and their respective allies from the mid-1940s until the early 1990s.
Capitalism	Capitalism generally refers to an economic system in which the means of production are mostly privately owned and operated for profit, and in which distribution, production and pricing of goods and services are determined in a largely free market. It is usually considered to involve the right of individuals and groups of individuals acting as "legal persons" or corporations to trade capital goods, labor, land and money.
Tariff	A tariff is a tax on foreign goods upon importation. When a ship arrives in port a customs officer inspects the contents and charges a tax according to the tariff formula. Since the goods cannot be landed until the tax is paid it is the easiest tax to collect, and the cost of collection is small. Smugglers of course seek to evade the tariff.
National security	National security refers to the requirement to maintain the survival of the nation-state through the use of economic, military and political power and the exercise of diplomacy.
Balance of trade	Balance of trade is the difference between the monetary value of exports and imports in an economy over a certain period of time.
Free market	A free market is a market where the price of an item is arranged by the mutual consent of sellers and buyers, with the supply and demand of that item not being regulated by a government; the opposite is a controlled market, where supply and price are set by a government.
Currency	A currency is a unit of exchange, facilitating the transfer of goods and services. It is a form of money, where money is an efficient medium of exchange, and it is also considered by several people as a store of value, created through a claim to its central bank assets.
Social welfare	A social welfare provision refers to any government program and which also seeks to provide a minimum level of income, service or other support for disadvantaged peoples such as the poor, elderly, disabled, students and minority groups.
Coalition	A coalition is an alliance among entities, during which they cooperate in joint action, each

Go to **Cram101.com** for the Practice Tests for this Chapter.

in their own self-interest. This alliance may be temporary or a matter of convenience. A coalition government, in a parliamentary system, is a government composed of a coalition of parties.

United Nations

The United Nations is an international organization whose stated aims are to facilitate co-operation in international law, international security, economic development, social progress and human rights issues.

Nationalization

Nationalization is the act of transferring assets into public ownership. It usually refers to the transfer of private assets, but may also mean assets owned by other levels of government, such as municipalities.

Lobbying

Lobbying is a concerted effort designed to achieve some result, typically from government authorities and elected officials. It can consist of the private cajoling of legislative members, public actions, or combinations of both public and private actions.

Pluralism

Pluralism is, in the general sense, the acknowledgment of diversity. The concept is used, often in different ways, in a wide range of issues. In politics, the affirmation of diversity in the interests of its citizens, and so political pluralism is one of the most important features of modern democracy.

Developed countries

The term developed countries is used to categorize countries with developed economies in which the tertiary and quaternary sectors of industry dominate. This level of economic development usually translates into a high income per capita and a high Human Development Index. Countries with high gross domestic product per capita often fit the above description of a developed economy.

Treaty

A treaty is an agreement under international law entered into by actors in international law, namely states and international organizations. Under United States constitutional law, only a treaty that has achieved advice and consent of two-thirds of the Senate present is properly designated as a treaty.

Subsidies

In economics, a subsidies is a kind of financial government assistance, such as a grant, tax break, or trade barrier, in order to encourage the production or purchase of a good. The term subsidy may also refer to assistance granted by others, such as individuals or non-government institutions, although this is more commonly described as charity.

Republic

A republic is a form of government maintained by a state or country whose sovereignty is based on popular consent and whose governance is based on popular representation and control. Several definitions stress the importance of the rule of law as among the requirements for a republic.

Central bank

A central bank is an entity responsible for the monetary policy of its country or of a group of member states. In most countries the central bank is state-owned and has a minimal degree of autonomy, which allows for the possibility of government intervening in monetary policy.

Referendum

A referendum is a direct vote in which an entire electorate is asked to either accept or reject a particular proposal. This may be the adoption of a new constitution, a constitutional amendment, a law, the recall of an elected official or simply a specific government policy. The referendum is a form of direct democracy.

Electorate

In politics, an electorate is the group of people entitled to vote in an election. The term can refer to:the totality of voters or electors the partisans of a particular individual, group or political party the collection of the voters enrolled in a geographically-defined area less commonly, the geographically-defined area which returns a representative.

Citizenship

Citizenship is membership in a political community and carries with it rights to political participation; a person having such membership is a citizen. It is largely coterminous with nationality, although it is possible to have a nationality without being a citizen ; it is

Go to **Cram101.com** for the Practice Tests for this Chapter.

67

also possible to have political rights without being a national of a state.

Monetary policy	Monetary policy is the process by which the government, central bank, or monetary authority manages the money supply to achieve specific goals—such as constraining inflation or deflation, maintaining an exchange rate, achieving full employment or economic growth.
Bureaucrat	A bureaucrat is a member of a bureaucracy, usually within an institution of the government.
Regional integration	Regional integration is a process in which states enter into a supranational regional organization in order to increase regional cooperation and diffuse regional tensions. Past efforts at regional integration have often focused on removing barriers to free trade in the region, increasing the free movement of people, labor, goods, and capital across national borders, reducing the possibility of regional armed conflict (for example, through Confidence and Security-Building Measures), and adopting cohesive regional stances on policy issues, such as the environment.
Legislation	Legislation is law which has been promulgated (or "enacted") by a legislature or other governing body. The term may refer to a single law, or the collective body of enacted law, while "statute" is also used to refer to a single law. Before an item of legislation becomes law it may be known as a bill, which is typically also known as "legislation" while it remains under active consideration.
Sovereignty	Sovereignty is the exclusive right to exercise supreme political authority over a geographic region, group of people, or oneself. The source or justification of sovereignty ("by God" or "by people") must be distinguished from its exercise by branches of government. In democratic states, sovereignty is held by the people.
Reciprocity	In international relations and treaties, the principle of reciprocity states that favours, benefits, or penalties that are granted by one state to the citizens or legal entities of another, should be returned in kind.
Trade organization	Trade organization is generally a public relations organization founded and funded by corporations that operate in a specific industry. Its purpose is generally to promote the industry through PR activities such as advertizing, education, political donations, lobbying and publishing.
World Trade Organization	World Trade Organization is an international organization designed to supervise and liberalize international trade. The WTO came into being on January 1, 1995, and is the successor to the General Agreement on Tariffs and Trade, which was created in 1947, and continued to operate for almost five decades as a de facto international organization.
Reconstruction	Reconstruction was the attempts from 1865 to 1877 in U.S. history to resolve the issues of the American Civil War, when both the Confederacy and slavery were destroyed. Reconstruction addressed the return of the Southern states that had seceded, the status of ex-Confederate leaders, and the Constitutional and legal status of the African-American Freedmen.
Private sector	The private sector of a nation's economy consists of enterprise that is outside the state. It includes a variety of for-profit entities such as private limited companies, partnerships, corporations, banks, as well as individuals not employed by the state.
Sustainable development	Sustainable development is defined by its proponents as balancing the fulfillment of human needs with the protection of the natural environment so that these needs can be met not only in the present, but in the indefinite future.
Bilateral	**Bilateral**ism is a term referring to political and cultural relations between two states. Most international diplomacy is done bilaterally. Examples of this include treaties between two countries, exchanges of ambassadors, and state visits. The alternatives to bilateral relations are multilateral relations, which involve many states, and unilateralism, when one state acts on its own.

Public administration	Public administration can be broadly described as the study and implementation of policy. As a moral endeavor, public administration is linked to pursuing the public good through the creation of civil society and social justice.
Authoritarianism	Authoritarianism describes a form of social control characterized by strict obedience to the authority of a state or organization, often maintaining and enforcing control through the use of oppressive measures.
Democracy	Democracy is a form of government in which supreme power is vested in the people and exercised by them directly or indirectly through a system of representation usually involving periodic free elections.
Jurisdiction	In law, jurisdiction is the practical authority granted to a formally constituted legal body or to a political leader to deal with and make pronouncements on legal matters and, by implication, to administer justice within a defined area of responsibility.
Economic Growth	Economic growth is the increase in value of the goods and services produced by an economy. It is conventionally measured as the percent rate of increase in real gross domestic product, or GDP. Growth is usually calculated in real terms, i.e. inflation-adjusted terms, in order to net out the effect of inflation on the price of the goods and services produced.
Imperialism	Imperialism is the policy of extending a nation's authority by territorial acquisition or by the establishment of economic and political hegemony over other nations, countries, or colonies. This is realized either through direct territorial conquest or settlement, or through indirect methods of influencing or controlling the politics and/or economy.
Prime minister	A prime minister is the most senior minister of a cabinet in the executive branch of government in a parliamentary system.
Caucus	A caucus is most generally defined as being a meeting of supporters or members of a political party or movement. The exact definition varies between many different countries.
Labor movement	Labor movement is a broad term for the development of a collective organization of working people, to campaign in their own interest for better treatment from their employers and political governments, in particular through the implementation of specific laws governing labor relations.
Confederation	A confederation is an association of sovereign states or communities, usually created by treaty but often later adopting a common constitution. Confederations tend to be established for dealing with critical issues, such as defense, foreign affairs, foreign trade, and a common currency, with the central government being required to provide support for all members.
Standard of living	The standard of living refers to the quality and quantity of goods and services available to people and the way these services and goods are distributed within a population. It is generally measured by standards such as income inequality, poverty rate, real income per person.
Bureaucracy	Bureaucracy is a concept in sociology and political science referring to the way that the administrative execution and enforcement of legal rules are socially organized. This office organization is characterized by standardized procedure, formal division of responsibility, hierarchy, and impersonal relationships.
Mandate	In international law, a mandate is a binding obligation issued from an inter-governmental organization like the United Nations to a country which is bound to follow the instructions of the organization.

United Nations	The United Nations is an international organization whose stated aims are to facilitate co-operation in international law, international security, economic development, social progress and human rights issues.
International relations	International relations a branch of political science, is the study of foreign relations and global issues among states within the international system, including the roles of states, inter-governmental organizations, non-governmental organizations, and multinational corporations. It is both an academic and public policy field, and can be either positive or normative as it both seeks to analyze as well as formulate the foreign policy of particular states.
Political economy	Political economy was the original term for the study of production, the acts of buying and selling, and their relationships to laws, customs and government. It developed in the 18th century as the study of the economies of states.
Peacekeeping	Peacekeeping, as defined by the United Nations, is "a way to help countries torn by conflict create conditions for sustainable peace.
Human rights	Human rights refers to universal rights of people regardless of jurisdiction or other factors, such as ethnicity, age, nationality, sexual orientation or religion.
Sustainable development	Sustainable development is defined by its proponents as balancing the fulfillment of human needs with the protection of the natural environment so that these needs can be met not only in the present, but in the indefinite future.
World Bank	The World Bank Group is a group of five international organizations responsible for providing finance and advice to countries for the purposes of economic development and eliminating poverty.
Globalization	Globalization is an umbrella term and is perhaps best understood as a unitary process inclusive of many sub-processes (such as enhanced economic interdependence, increased cultural influence, rapid advances of information technology, and novel governance and geopolitical challenges) that are increasingly binding people and the biosphere more tightly into one global system.
Sovereignty	Sovereignty is the exclusive right to exercise supreme political authority over a geographic region, group of people, or oneself. The source or justification of sovereignty ("by God" or "by people") must be distinguished from its exercise by branches of government. In democratic states, sovereignty is held by the people.
Rule of law	The rule of law is the principle that governmental authority is legitimately exercized only in accordance with written, publicly disclosed laws adopted and enforced in accordance with established procedure.
Law and order	In politics, law and order refers to a political platform which supports a strict criminal justice system, especially in relation to violent crime and property crime, through harsher criminal penalties. These penalties may include longer terms of imprisonment, mandatory sentencing, and in some countries, capital punishment.
Status quo	Status quo is a Latin termpresent, current, existing state of affairs. To maintain the status quo is to keep the things the way they presently are. The related phrase status quo ante, means "the state of things as it was before."
Legislature	A legislature is a type of representative deliberative assembly with the power to adopt laws. In presidential systems of government, the legislature is considered a power branch which is equal to, and independent of, the executive.
Judiciary	In the law, the judiciary is the system of courts which administer justice in the name of the sovereign or state, a mechanism for the resolution of disputes.The term is also used to refer

Go to **Cram101.com** for the Practice Tests for this Chapter.

	collectively to the judges, magistrates and other adjudicators who form the core of a judiciary, as well as the support personnel who keep the system running smoothly.
Jurisdiction	In law, jurisdiction is the practical authority granted to a formally constituted legal body or to a political leader to deal with and make pronouncements on legal matters and, by implication, to administer justice within a defined area of responsibility.
Anarchism	Anarchism is a political philosophy or group of doctrines and attitudes centered on rejection of any form of compulsory government and supporting its elimination. Thus anarchism, in its most general meaning, is the belief that all forms of rulership and thus also involuntary servitude are undesirable and should be abolished.
Diplomacy	Diplomacy is the art and practice of conducting negotiations between representatives of groups or states. It usually refers to international diplomacy, the conduct of international relations through the intercession of professional diplomats with regard to issues of peace-making, trade, war, economics and culture. International treaties are usually negotiated by diplomats prior to endorsement by national politicians.
Treaty	A treaty is an agreement under international law entered into by actors in international law, namely states and international organizations. Under United States constitutional law, only a treaty that has achieved advice and consent of two-thirds of the Senate present is properly designated as a treaty.
Ratification	Ratification is the act of giving official sanction to a formal document such as a treaty or constitution. It includes the process of adopting an international treaty by the legislature, a constitution, or another nationally binding document by the agreement of multiple sub-national entities.
Corporation	A corporation is an artificial legal entity which, while made up of a number of natural persons or other legal entities, has a separate legal identity from them. As a legal entity the corporation receives legal rights and duties
Multinational corporation	A multinational corporation is a corporation or enterprise that manages production establishments or delivers services in at least two countries. Very large multinationals have budgets that exceed those of many countries. They can have a powerful influence in international relations and local economies.
Genocide	Genocide is the mass killing of a group of people as defined by Article 2 of the Convention on the Prevention and Punishment of the Crime of Genocide (CPPCG) as "any of the following acts committed with intent to destroy, in whole or in part, a national, ethnical, racial or religious group, as such: killing members of the group; causing serious bodily or mental harm to members of the group; deliberately inflicting on the group conditions of life, calculated to bring about its physical destruction in whole or in part; imposing measures intended to prevent births within the group; and forcibly transferring children of the group to another group."
Reprisal	In warfare, a reprisal is a limited and deliberate violation of the laws of war to punish an enemy for breaking the laws of war. A legally executed reprisal is not an atrocity.
Collective action	Collective action is the pursuit of a goal or set of goals by more than one person. It is a term which has formulations and theories in many areas of the social sciences.
Collective security	Collective Security is a system aspiring to the maintenance of peace, in which participants agree that any "breach of the peace is to be declared to be of concern to all the participating states," 1 and will result in a collective response. This began in 1918 after the international balance of power was perceived by many nations to be no longer working correctly.
Federalism	Federalism is a political philosophy in which a group of members are bound together with a

Chapter 9. The Quest for Global Governance

Go to **Cram101.com** for the Practice Tests for this Chapter.
And, **NEVER** highlight a book again!

	governing representative head. The term federalism is also used to describe a system of government in which sovereignty is constitutionally divided between a central governing authority and constituent political units.
Functionalism	**Functionalism** is a theory of international relations that arose principally from the experience of the Second World War and a strong concern about the obsolescence of the State as a form of social organisation. Rather than the self-interest of nation-states that realists see as a motivating factor, functionalists focus on common interests and needs shared by states.
Nationalism	Nationalism, in its broadest sense, is a devotion to one's own nation and its interests over those of all other nations. The term can also refer to a doctrine or political movement that holds that a nation—usually defined in terms of ethnicity or culture—has the right to constitute an independent or autonomous political community based on a shared history and common destiny.
Tariff	A tariff is a tax on foreign goods upon importation. When a ship arrives in port a customs officer inspects the contents and charges a tax according to the tariff formula. Since the goods cannot be landed until the tax is paid it is the easiest tax to collect, and the cost of collection is small. Smugglers of course seek to evade the tariff.
National security	National security refers to the requirement to maintain the survival of the nation-state through the use of economic, military and political power and the exercise of diplomacy.
Tragedy of the commons	The tragedy of the commons is a type of social trap that involves a conflict over resources between individual interests and the common good.
World government	World government is the concept of a political body that would make, interpret and enforce international law. Inherent to the concept of a world government is the idea that nations would be required to pool or surrender sovereignty over some areas.
Police power	Police power is the capacity of a state to regulate behaviors and enforce order within its territory, often framed in terms of public welfare, security, morality, and safety. Police power is legally considered an inherent right, and is limited only by prohibitions specified in the constitution of a state, making it the most expansive authority exercized by a state.
Trade organization	Trade organization is generally a public relations organization founded and funded by corporations that operate in a specific industry. Its purpose is generally to promote the industry through PR activities such as advertizing, education, political donations, lobbying and publishing.
World Trade Organization	World Trade Organization is an international organization designed to supervise and liberalize international trade. The WTO came into being on January 1, 1995, and is the successor to the General Agreement on Tariffs and Trade, which was created in 1947, and continued to operate for almost five decades as a de facto international organization.
Regime	A regime is the set of rules, both formal and informal that regulate the operation of government and its interactions with the economy and society.
Foreign policy	A country's foreign policy is a set of political goals that seeks to outline how that particular country will interact with other countries of the world and, to a lesser extent, non-state actors. They generally are designed to help protect a country's national interests, national security, ideological goals, and economic prosperity.
Refugee	A refugee is a person who is seeking asylum in a foreign country in order to escape persecution, war, terrorism, extreme poverty, famines, and natural disaster. Some regional legal instruments further include those seeking to escape generalized violence in the definition of a refugee.

Go to **Cram101.com** for the Practice Tests for this Chapter.

Bilateral	**Bilateral**ism is a term referring to political and cultural relations between two states. Most international diplomacy is done bilaterally. Examples of this include treaties between two countries, exchanges of ambassadors, and state visits. The alternatives to bilateral relations are multilateral relations, which involve many states, and unilateralism, when one state acts on its own.
Delegate	A delegate is an individual or a member of a group called at the interests of a larger organization at a meeting of some kind. In order to avoid the principal-agent problem, it is generally important to the organization to take steps to ensure that the delegate does not have a conflict of interest.
Cuban Missile Crisis	The Cuban Missile Crisis was a confrontation during the Cold War between the Government of the United States, the Government of the Soviet Union, and the Government of Cuba. This crisis is generally regarded as the moment when the Cold War came closest to escalating into a nuclear war.
Mandate	In international law, a mandate is a binding obligation issued from an inter-governmental organization like the United Nations to a country which is bound to follow the instructions of the organization.
Arbitration	Arbitration is a legal technique for the resolution of disputes outside the courts, wherein the parties to a dispute refer it to one or more persons (the "arbitrators" or "arbitral tribunal"), by whose decision they agree to be bound. In the United States and other countries, the term is sometimes used in the context of describing alternative dispute resolution, a category that more commonly refers to mediation (a form of settlement negotiation facilitated by a neutral third party).
Referendum	A referendum is a direct vote in which an entire electorate is asked to either accept or reject a particular proposal. This may be the adoption of a new constitution, a constitutional amendment, a law, the recall of an elected official or simply a specific government policy. The referendum is a form of direct democracy.
Humanitarianism	Humanitarianism is an informal ideology of practice, whereby people practice humane treatment and provide assistance to others.
Veto	Veto is used to denote that a certain party has the right to stop unilaterally a certain piece of legislation. A veto gives power, possibly unlimited, to stop changes, but not to adopt them.
International Monetary Fund	The International Monetary Fund is an international organization that oversees the global financial system by observing exchange rates and balance of payments, as well as offering financial and technical assistance. Its headquarters are located in Washington, D.C., USA.
Cold War	The Cold War was the period of conflict, tension and competition between the United States and the Soviet Union and their respective allies from the mid-1940s until the early 1990s.
Social welfare	A social welfare provision refers to any government program and which also seeks to provide a minimum level of income, service or other support for disadvantaged peoples such as the poor, elderly, disabled, students and minority groups.
Welfare	Welfare is financial assistance paid by taxpayers to groups of people who are unable to support themselves, and determined to be able to function more effectively with financial assistance.
Disarmament	**Disarmament** means the act of reducing or depriving arms i.e. weaponry. Disarmament can be contrasted with "arms control," which essentially refers to the act of "controlling arms," rather than eliminating them.
Initiative	In political science, the initiative provides a means by which a petition signed by a certain

minimum number of registered voters can force a public vote on a proposed statute, constitutional amendment, charter amendment or ordinance, or, in its minimal form, to simply oblige the executive or legislative bodies to consider the subject by submitting it to the order of the day.

Autonomy	Autonomy means freedom from external authority. In politics, autonomy refers to self-governance.
Legitimacy	Legitimacy in political science, is the popular acceptance of a governing regime or law as an authority. Where as authority refers to a specific position in an established government, the term legitimacy is used when describing a system of government itself —where "government may be generalized to mean the wider "sphere of influence."
Preventive diplomacy	Preventive diplomacy is action to prevent disputes from arizing between parties, to prevent existing disputes from escalating into conflicts and to limit the spread of the latter when they occur.
Legislation	Legislation is law which has been promulgated (or "enacted") by a legislature or other governing body. The term may refer to a single law, or the collective body of enacted law, while "statute" is also used to refer to a single law. Before an item of legislation becomes law it may be known as a bill, which is typically also known as "legislation" while it remains under active consideration.
Internationalism	Internationalism is a political movement which advocates a greater economic and political cooperation among nations for the benefit of all. Partisans of this movement, such as supporters of the World Federalist Movement, claim that nations should cooperate because their long-term mutual interests are of greater value than their individual short-term needs.
Balance of power	Balance of power refers to the division, distribution, or separation of powers within a national political system.
Deterrence	Deterrence theory is a military strategy developed after and used throughout the Cold War and current times. It is especially relevant with regard to the use of nuclear weapons, and figures prominently on current United States foreign policy regarding the development of nuclear technology in North Korea and Iran.
Constituency	The most common meaning of constituency occurs in politics and means either the group of people from whom an individual or organization hopes to attract support, or the group of people or geographical area that a particular elected representative or group of elected representatives represents.
Representation	In politics, representation describes how residents of a country are empowered in the government. Representation usually refers to representative democracies, where elected representatives speak for their constituents in the legislature. Generally, only citizens are granted representation in the government in the form of voting rights, however some democracies have extended this right further.
Fourth World	The term Fourth World was coined by Manuel Castells to refer to black holes of social exclusion. Fourth World is deliberately opposed to First World, Second World and Third World, all of which imply a certain degree of connectivity. This connectivity is what is notably absent in the notion of Fourth World.
Economism	Economism is a term used to criticize economic reductionism, that is the reduction of all social facts to economical dimensions. It is also used to criticize economics as an ideology, in which supply and demand are the only important factors in decisions, and literally outstrip or permit ignoring all other factors.
New International	The New International Economic Order (NIEO) was a set of proposals put forward during the 1970s by developing countries through the United Nations Conference on Trade and Development

Economic Order	to promote their interests by improving their terms of trade, increasing development assistance, developed-country tariff reductions, and other means.
Developed countries	The term developed countries is used to categorize countries with developed economies in which the tertiary and quaternary sectors of industry dominate. This level of economic development usually translates into a high income per capita and a high Human Development Index. Countries with high gross domestic product per capita often fit the above description of a developed economy.
Free trade	Free trade is a market model in which trade in goods and services between or within countries flows unhindered by government-imposed restrictions. Restrictions to trade include taxes and other legislation, such as tariff and non-tariff trade barriers.
World Wide Web	World Wide Web is a system of interlinked, hypertext documents accessed via the Internet. With a Web browser, a user views Web pages that may contain text, images, and other multimedia and navigates between them using hyperlinks.
Civil society	Civil society is composed of the totality of voluntary civic and social organizations and institutions that form the basis of a functioning society as opposed to the force-backed structures of a state (regardless of that state's political system) and commercial institutions.
Reasons of state	The reasons of state is a country's goals and ambitions whether economic, military, or cultural. The notion is an important one in international relations where pursuit of the national interest is the foundation of the realist school.
Democracy	Democracy is a form of government in which supreme power is vested in the people and exercised by them directly or indirectly through a system of representation usually involving periodic free elections.
Public good	In economics, a public good is a good that is non-rivalrous. This means: consumption of the good by one individual does not reduce the amount of the good available for consumption by others. For example, if one individual eats a cake, there is no cake left for anyone else; but breathing air or drinking water from a stream does not significantly reduce the amount of air or water available to others.
Public goods	In economics, a public goods is a good that is non-rivalrous and non-excludable. This means: consumption of the good by one individual does not reduce the amount of the good available for consumption by others; and no one can be effectively excluded from using that good.

Human rights	Human rights refers to universal rights of people regardless of jurisdiction or other factors, such as ethnicity, age, nationality, sexual orientation or religion.
International relations	International relations a branch of political science, is the study of foreign relations and global issues among states within the international system, including the roles of states, inter-governmental organizations, non-governmental organizations, and multinational corporations. It is both an academic and public policy field, and can be either positive or normative as it both seeks to analyze as well as formulate the foreign policy of particular states.
Corporation	A corporation is an artificial legal entity which, while made up of a number of natural persons or other legal entities, has a separate legal identity from them. As a legal entity the corporation receives legal rights and duties
Multinational corporation	A multinational corporation is a corporation or enterprise that manages production establishments or delivers services in at least two countries. Very large multinationals have budgets that exceed those of many countries. They can have a powerful influence in international relations and local economies.
Civil society	Civil society is composed of the totality of voluntary civic and social organizations and institutions that form the basis of a functioning society as opposed to the force-backed structures of a state (regardless of that state's political system) and commercial institutions.
Political economy	Political economy was the original term for the study of production, the acts of buying and selling, and their relationships to laws, customs and government. It developed in the 18th century as the study of the economies of states.
Terrorism	As a form of unconventional warfare, terrorism is sometimes used when attempting to force political change by: convincing a government or population to agree to demands to avoid future harm or fear of harm, destabilization of an existing government, motivating a disgruntled population to join an uprizing, escalating a conflict in the hopes of disrupting the status quo, expressing a grievance, or drawing attention to a cause.
Globalization	Globalization is an umbrella term and is perhaps best understood as a unitary process inclusive of many sub-processes (such as enhanced economic interdependence, increased cultural influence, rapid advances of information technology, and novel governance and geopolitical challenges) that are increasingly binding people and the biosphere more tightly into one global system.
Sovereignty	Sovereignty is the exclusive right to exercise supreme political authority over a geographic region, group of people, or oneself. The source or justification of sovereignty ("by God" or "by people") must be distinguished from its exercise by branches of government. In democratic states, sovereignty is held by the people.
Balance of power	Balance of power refers to the division, distribution, or separation of powers within a national political system.
United Nations	The United Nations is an international organization whose stated aims are to facilitate co-operation in international law, international security, economic development, social progress and human rights issues.
Deforestation	Deforestation is the conversion of forested areas to non-forest land use such as arable land, pasture, urban use, logged area or wasteland.
Developed countries	The term developed countries is used to categorize countries with developed economies in which the tertiary and quaternary sectors of industry dominate. This level of economic development usually translates into a high income per capita and a high Human Development Index. Countries with high gross domestic product per capita often fit the above description

Go to **Cram101.com** for the Practice Tests for this Chapter.

of a developed economy.

Standard of living	The standard of living refers to the quality and quantity of goods and services available to people and the way these services and goods are distributed within a population. It is generally measured by standards such as income inequality, poverty rate, real income per person.
World Bank	The World Bank Group is a group of five international organizations responsible for providing finance and advice to countries for the purposes of economic development and eliminating poverty.
Sustainable development	Sustainable development is defined by its proponents as balancing the fulfillment of human needs with the protection of the natural environment so that these needs can be met not only in the present, but in the indefinite future.
Imperialism	Imperialism is the policy of extending a nation's authority by territorial acquisition or by the establishment of economic and political hegemony over other nations, countries, or colonies. This is realized either through direct territorial conquest or settlement, or through indirect methods of influencing or controlling the politics and/or economy.
Global warming	**Global warming** is the increase in the average temperature of the Earth's near-surface air and oceans in recent decades and its projected continuation.
Industrializ-tion	Industrialisation (also spelt **Industrialization**) or an Industrial Revolution is a process of social and economic change whereby a human society is transformed from a pre-industrial to an industrial state.
Economic Growth	Economic growth is the increase in value of the goods and services produced by an economy. It is conventionally measured as the percent rate of increase in real gross domestic product, or GDP. Growth is usually calculated in real terms, i.e. inflation-adjusted terms, in order to net out the effect of inflation on the price of the goods and services produced.
Economism	Economism is a term used to criticize economic reductionism, that is the reduction of all social facts to economical dimensions. It is also used to criticize economics as an ideology, in which supply and demand are the only important factors in decisions, and literally outstrip or permit ignoring all other factors.
State action	A state action is a term used in United States civil rights law to describe a person who is acting on behalf of a governmental body, and is therefore subject to regulation under the United States bill of rights including the First, Fifth and Fourteenth Amendments, which prohibit the federal and state governments from violating certain rights and freedoms.
Treaty	A treaty is an agreement under international law entered into by actors in international law, namely states and international organizations. Under United States constitutional law, only a treaty that has achieved advice and consent of two-thirds of the Senate present is properly designated as a treaty.
Civil rights	Civil rights are the protections and privileges of personal power given to all citizens by law. Civil rights are distinguished from "human rights" or "natural rights", also called "our God-given rights". They are rights that are bestowed by nations on those within their territorial boundaries, while natural or human rights are rights that many scholars claim should belong to all people.
Natural rights	Natural rights are universal rights that are seen as inherent in the nature of people and not contingent on human actions or beliefs. One theory of natural rights was developed from the theory of natural law during the Enlightenment in opposition to the divine right of kings, and provided a moral justification for liberalism.
Bill of Rights	A bill of rights is a list or summary of which is considered important and essential by a

	group of people. The purpose of these bills is to protect those rights against infringement by other people and the government.
Constitution	A constitution is a system that establishes the rules and principles that govern an organization or political entity.
Due process	In United States law, adopted from English Law, due process is the principle that the government must normally respect all of a person's legal rights instead of just some or most of those legal rights when the government deprives a person of life, liberty, or property. Due process has also been frequently interpreted as placing limitations on laws and legal proceedings, in order for judges instead of legislators to guarantee fundamental fairness, justice, and liberty.
Free Press	Free Press is a non-partisan, non-profit organization founded by media critic Robert McChesney to promote more democratic media policy in the United States.
Welfare	Welfare is financial assistance paid by taxpayers to groups of people who are unable to support themselves, and determined to be able to function more effectively with financial assistance.
Social welfare	A social welfare provision refers to any government program and which also seeks to provide a minimum level of income, service or other support for disadvantaged peoples such as the poor, elderly, disabled, students and minority groups.
Social Security	Social security primarily refers to a field of social welfare service concerned with social protection, or protection against socially recognized conditions, including poverty, old age, disability, unemployment, families with children and others. Although some publications use the terms "social security" and "social protection" interchangeably, social security is used both more narrowly and more widely.
Democracy	Democracy is a form of government in which supreme power is vested in the people and exercised by them directly or indirectly through a system of representation usually involving periodic free elections.
Civil liberties	Civil liberties is the name given to freedoms that completely protect the individual from government. Civil liberties set limits for government so that it can not abuse its power and interfere with the lives of its citizens.
Republic	A republic is a form of government maintained by a state or country whose sovereignty is based on popular consent and whose governance is based on popular representation and control. Several definitions stress the importance of the rule of law as among the requirements for a republic.
Holocaust	The **Holocaust** , also known as Ha-Shoah, Khurbn or Halokaust, is the term generally used to describe the killing of approximately six million European Jews during World War II, as part of a program of deliberate extermination planned and executed by the National Socialist regime in Germany led by Adolf Hitler.
Genocide	Genocide is the mass killing of a group of people as defined by Article 2 of the Convention on the Prevention and Punishment of the Crime of Genocide (CPPCG) as "any of the following acts committed with intent to destroy, in whole or in part, a national, ethnical, racial or religious group, as such: killing members of the group; causing serious bodily or mental harm to members of the group; deliberately inflicting on the group conditions of life, calculated to bring about its physical destruction in whole or in part; imposing measures intended to prevent births within the group; and forcibly transferring children of the group to another group."
Reasons of state	The reasons of state is a country's goals and ambitions whether economic, military, or cultural. The notion is an important one in international relations where pursuit of the

Go to **Cram101.com** for the Practice Tests for this Chapter.

national interest is the foundation of the realist school.

National security	National security refers to the requirement to maintain the survival of the nation-state through the use of economic, military and political power and the exercise of diplomacy.
Initiative	In political science, the initiative provides a means by which a petition signed by a certain minimum number of registered voters can force a public vote on a proposed statute, constitutional amendment, charter amendment or ordinance, or, in its minimal form, to simply oblige the executive or legislative bodies to consider the subject by submitting it to the order of the day.
Direct action	Direct action is a form of political activism which seeks immediate remedy for perceived ills, as opposed to indirect actions such as electing representatives who promise to provide remedy at some later date. Direct action can include such activities as strikes, workplace occupations, sabotage, sit-ins, squatting, revolutionary/guerrilla warfare, demonstrations, vandalism or graffiti.
Economic sanction	A economic sanction is a economic penalty applied by one country on another for a variety of reasons. They include, but are not limited to, tariffs, trade barriers, import duties, and import or export quotas.
Weapons of mass destruction	Weapons of mass destruction is a term used to describe a massive weapon with the capacity to indiscriminately kill large numbers of people. The phrase broadly encompasses several areas of weapon synthesis, including nuclear, biological, chemical and, increasingly, radiological weapons.
Regime	A regime is the set of rules, both formal and informal that regulate the operation of government and its interactions with the economy and society.
Political culture	Political culture is a distinctive and patterned form of political philosophy that consists of beliefs on how governmental, political, and economic life should be carried out. Political culture creates a frame work ofr political change and are unique to nations, states, and other groups.
Humanitarianism	Humanitarianism is an informal ideology of practice, whereby people practice humane treatment and provide assistance to others.
Lobbying	Lobbying is a concerted effort designed to achieve some result, typically from government authorities and elected officials. It can consist of the private cajoling of legislative members, public actions, or combinations of both public and private actions.
World Wide Web	World Wide Web is a system of interlinked, hypertext documents accessed via the Internet. With a Web browser, a user views Web pages that may contain text, images, and other multimedia and navigates between them using hyperlinks.
Constituency	The most common meaning of constituency occurs in politics and means either the group of people from whom an individual or organization hopes to attract support, or the group of people or geographical area that a particular elected representative or group of elected representatives represents.
Suffrage	Suffrage is the civil right to vote, or the exercise of that right. Universal suffrage is the term used to describe a situation in which the right to vote is not restricted by race, sex, belief or social status.
Division of labor	Division of labor is the specialisation of cooperative labor in specific, circumscribed tasks and roles, intended to increase efficiency of output. Historically the growth of a more and more complex division of labor is closely associated with the growth of trade, the rise of capitalism, and of the complexity of industrialisation processes.
Autonomy	Autonomy means freedom from external authority. In politics, autonomy refers to self-

governance.

Coalition	A coalition is an alliance among entities, during which they cooperate in joint action, each in their own self-interest. This alliance may be temporary or a matter of convenience. A coalition government, in a parliamentary system, is a government composed of a coalition of parties.
Radicalism	Radicalism is a political movement for those favouring or trying to produce thoroughgoing political reforms which can include changes to the social order to a greater or lesser extent toward the right.
Tragedy of the commons	The tragedy of the commons is a type of social trap that involves a conflict over resources between individual interests and the common good.
Diplomacy	Diplomacy is the art and practice of conducting negotiations between representatives of groups or states. It usually refers to international diplomacy, the conduct of international relations through the intercession of professional diplomats with regard to issues of peace-making, trade, war, economics and culture. International treaties are usually negotiated by diplomats prior to endorsement by national politicians.
Anarchism	Anarchism is a political philosophy or group of doctrines and attitudes centered on rejection of any form of compulsory government and supporting its elimination. Thus anarchism, in its most general meaning, is the belief that all forms of rulership and thus also involuntary servitude are undesirable and should be abolished.
Arms control	Arms control is an umbrella term for restrictions upon the development, production, stockpiling, proliferation, and usage of weapons, especially weapons of mass destruction. Arms control is typically exercised through the use of diplomacy which seeks to impose such limitations upon consenting participants through international treaties and agreements, although it may also comprise efforts by a nation or group of nations to enforce limitations upon a non-consenting country.
Balance of payments	Balance of payments measures the payments that flow between any individual country and all other countries. It is used to summarize all international economic transactions for that country during a specific time period, usually a year. The Balance of payments is determined by the country's exports and imports of goods, services, and financial capital, as well as financial transfers. It reflects all payments and liabilities to foreigners (debits) and all payments and obligations received from foreigners (credits).
Behavioralism	Behavioralism is an approach in political science which seeks to provide an objective, quantified approach to explaining and predicting political behavior. It is associated with the rise of the behavioral sciences, modeled after the natural sciences.

Go to **Cram101.com** for the Practice Tests for this Chapter.

CPSIA information can be obtained
at www.ICGtesting.com
Printed in the USA
FSHW011141010219
55411FS